Measuring
the Success of
Employee
Engagement

A Step-by-Step Guide for Measuring Impact and Calculating ROI

PRESS

ROI INSTITUTE™

Patricia Pulliam Phillips, PhD
Jack J. Phillips, PhD
Rebecca Ray, PhD

19 18 17 16   1 2 3 4 5

Chapter 1 was originally published as "Engage Employees at Work: Changing the Nature of Work to Maximize Performance," chap. 6 in *High-Impact Human Capital Strategy* (New York: AMACOM, 2015), and is adapted with permission.

ATD Press is an internationally renowned source of insightful and practical information on talent development, training, and professional development.

ATD Press
1640 King Street
Alexandria, VA 22314 USA

Ordering information: Books published by ATD Press can be purchased by visiting ATD's website at www.td.org/books or by calling 800.628.2783 or 703.683.8100.

Library of Congress Control Number: 2016932260

ISBN-10: 1-56286-918-3
ISBN-13: 978-1-56286-918-2
e-ISBN: 978-1-60728-009-5

ATD Press Editorial Staff:
Director: Kristine Luecker
Manager: Christian Green
Community of Practice Manager, Senior Leaders & Executives: Ann Parker
Associate Editor: Melissa Jones
Text and Cover Design: Iris Sanchez

Printed by Versa Press, Inc., East Peoria, IL

Table of Contents

Preface

A large construction aggregates company with 300 plants was facing a typical challenge. Although it was successful, there was an opportunity to improve. In a low-cost industry, the company struggled to keep operating costs below the target numbers. However, company executives believed that if employees were more engaged, plant-operating costs should be reduced. A survey was administered to confirm the status of engagement, and the results were much lower than expected. The employee engagement system needed to be revised. The vice president of operations agreed, and approved a project that involved:

- adjustments in job descriptions and responsibilities
- a revision of the definition of engagement
- formal training with employees and plant managers
- sharing cost data with employees
- brainstorming sessions with employees to generate cost-saving ideas
- routine meetings with employees to discuss actions
- a gainsharing program that shared half the cost savings with employees.

The project would be implemented on a pilot basis with six plants. If successful, it would be implemented in all plants at a cost of about $12 million. The VP of operations was willing to make this investment if the human resource function could show the financial return on investment (ROI)—"How can I spend this amount of money and not show my shareholders the return on this investment?" This request presented a challenge to the HR executives, who had never pursued an ROI study for any of their previous projects.

This case study highlights three developing trends:

- Globally, a record amount of money is being invested in employee engagement, as confirmed by several benchmarking reports.
- A record number of requests are being made for accountability for employee engagement, including showing impact and ROI for major programs.
- Human resource professionals, particularly those involved in these soft skill areas, must be prepared to step up to this challenge, not only when impact and ROI are requested, but ideally before the request is made. HR professionals around the world are doing just that by developing the skills to become certified ROI professionals (CRP).

This case study has a happy ending, as detailed in chapter 8 of this book.

SNEAK PREVIEW

Measuring the Success of Employee Engagement addresses the issues outlined in the case study. It demonstrates how employee engagement can be evaluated, including measuring impact and ROI. This method represents a significant change in employee engagement because this process begins with the end in mind—the business impact, if it is evaluated at that level. This shift in thinking about employee engagement, which often begins with seeking new engagement behaviors, moves the discussion to business improvement. New behaviors are sought and needed for a reason, which often involves driving the impact of a group of people.

This book will take you through the necessary steps to make this development, and points to other resources for more detail if necessary. The information in the first half is complemented by the case studies in the second part, which use real-life examples to amplify how this challenge is being met. *Measuring the Success of Employee Engagement* is an essential resource for the employee engagement team, chief learning officer, chief talent officer, chief human resources officer, and others who support employee engagement.

THE FLOW OF THE BOOK

This book begins with a chapter about the status of employee engagement and the challenge of showing its worth to the organization. The next six chapters present the ROI Methodology, which is the most documented and used evaluation system in the world, and fits perfectly with employee engagement. Many practitioners are using this approach to clearly show the value of employee engagement using data that top executives appreciate and understand. Part II presents case studies that offer a variety of settings, programs, and content.

TARGET AUDIENCE

The principal audience for this book is individuals involved in leading the human resource or the learning and development function. Whether their title is chief learning officer, chief talent officer, or chief human resources officer, these individuals need to understand that major employee engagement programs are not only necessary, but can also provide impressive business results. When this value is shown, it improves support, respect, and critical funding for future employee engagement programs.

A second audience is employee engagement directors, organizers, coordinators, and consultants charged with implementing employee engagement in organizations. These practitioners need to know how to set up employee engagement programs to deliver value from the beginning, how to keep the focus on the business impact throughout the process, how to follow up to see if the business impact has been delivered, and how to show the financial ROI directly from the employee engagement program.

A third audience is individuals who are involved in or support employee engagement in some way. This group includes the participants of the program, managers who have some of their own team involved, advisers to the employee engagement team, employee engagement facilitators, external consultants and designers, and developers of employee engagement programs. For individuals in any of these roles, this book provides further evidence that employee engagement is making a difference and satisfying the appetites of the executive group.

CASE STUDIES

The case studies presented here represent a cross section of employee engagement programs with different levels of participants and in different types of organizational settings, such as manufacturing, construction, mining, retail stores, and hotels.

ACKNOWLEDGMENTS

Rebecca Ray

I remain deeply appreciative of the opportunity to continue the important discussion about the role and impact of employee engagement, this time through the detailed examination of real challenges and solutions articulated in this book. A special thanks to the executives who shared their stories with us and who see employee engagement—lifting people to their highest potential and ensuring the continued success of an organization—as a noble calling. Over the years, the leaders I've worked with, the teams I've been part of, and the challenges I've had the good fortune to tackle have taught me many things, some of them about the subject matter, but many more of them about myself as a leader. One of my greatest professional pleasures is to partner with Jack and Patti—their insights make me smarter, their ability to inspire thousands to tackle and master a sometimes daunting challenge is humbling, and their generosity of spirit is boundless. I am very fortunate. How often does one get an opportunity to learn from legends? Finally, I wish to thank my muse.

Patti and Jack

We want to thank all the leaders we have worked with during the last 23 years in our work at ROI Institute. Most of our projects take us to the middle and top leadership teams of organizations. We have had the pleasure of working with thousands of organizations and have witnessed the great results from many types of programs. The successful implementation of ROI in an organization is a direct result of great leadership for that function. We have seen firsthand that leaders can make a positive difference, and that they add value. We thank them for their efforts and applaud their accomplishments.

We also would like to acknowledge the great work of Rebecca Ray, executive vice president, knowledge organization and human capital lead at The Conference Board. Rebecca is an outstanding leader, who has led teams for learning and development and human resources in very high-profile organizations. She is also an outstanding teacher, speaker, writer, and researcher. She brings those skill sets quite effectively to The Conference Board. We are delighted to be working with her on another publication.

From Jack: Thanks to Patti, who inspires me to do my best as she keeps the team on track. She is an outstanding facilitator, an insightful consultant, a sought-after speaker, a meticulous writer, a prolific researcher, and most of all—a loving spouse.

From Patti: As always, much love and thanks go to Jack. You invest much more than you get in return. What a contribution you make! Thank you for your inspiration and the fun you bring to my life.

Finally, we want to thank the efforts of Hope Nicholas, director of publications for ROI Institute. Hope manages a very hectic schedule as we produce eight to 10 books each year with major publishers. Her great work shines through in this manuscript; we are fortunate to have her with us and are delighted to work with her again on another project. For this project, Hope was assisted by Anita Azeta, client relationship manager at ROI Institute.

Comments and Suggestions

As always, we welcome your comments, suggestions, and recommendations. This is the sixth book in the Measuring the Success of series and we have many more planned. Please send your thoughts directly to the authors or to ROI Institute at info@roiinstitute.net.

Patti Phillips
patti@roiinstitute.net

Jack Phillips
jack@roiinstitute.net

Rebecca Ray
Rebecca.Ray@conference-board.org

Birmingham, Alabama, and New York, New York

Part I
The ROI Methodology
A Credible Approach to Evaluating
Employee Engagement

1
The Importance of Employee Engagement

There is probably no other topic more frequently discussed in the human resources area than employee engagement. Articles, conferences, and books are filled with issues about employee engagement, usually for good reason. Fully engaged employees remain with their organization, produce more, and are more efficient. In addition, they will satisfy customers and increase sales. This is achieved by examining not only the *why, what,* and *how* of the work, but also *where* and *when* the work is done, addressing alternative and flexible work systems and workspace design. When these issues are addressed properly, they can foster a long-lasting, high-performing work team. This chapter explores a variety of issues about employee engagement, how to make it successful, and how to know when it is successful. It also discusses different arrangements for alternative and flexible work systems and how to make them successful—all leading toward a particular set of strategies for these issues.

THE SHIFTING NATURE OF WORK

When you look into any kind of organization, you can see that the nature of work has changed. In some organizations, it has changed dramatically, particularly for knowledge workers in office spaces. This change in work involves the work itself, the meaning of work, and how it is accomplished, including the place, time, and environment in which it is accomplished. This shift is illustrated in Exhibit 1-1, which shows the drastic differences between employee behaviors of the past and the future. Many of these changes focus on engagement—having an employee who is more connected to the organization—and that feeling of belonging and ownership translates into more effort, more productivity, and more success for both the individual and the organization (Morgan 2014). These issues represent important opportunities for change and improvement.

EXHIBIT 1-1. The Shifting Nature of Employees at Work

Past	Future
Disengaged with work	Engaged
Keep busy	Get Results
Find satisfaction away from work	Find satisfaction at work

3

EXHIBIT 1-1. The Shifting Nature of Employees at Work (continued)

Past	Future
Hoard information	Share information
No ownership of work	High levels of ownership
Focus on knowledge	Focus on adaptive learning
Minimal collaboration	High levels of collaboration
Predefined work	Customized work
No voice	Can be a leader
Focus on inputs	Focus on outcome
Work in a cube	Work in a variety of open space formats
Rely on email	Rely on collaboration technologies
Use company equipment	Uses many devices
Work 8-5	Work anytime
Work in the office	Work anywhere

Adapted from Morgan (2014).

Employee Engagement Is the Critical Difference

We've seen the headlines from newspapers in the developed economies of the United States and Europe about anemic economic growth, massive layoffs, scarce job openings, and worker disillusionment due to the demise of the "employee contract." Those still working often find themselves in an environment characterized by company instability, frequent management turnover, reductions in health benefits, reduction or elimination of pension contributions, and high levels of stress that result from the fear of losing a job or having to shoulder the burden of additional work left by departed coworkers. Those who find a new job after long-term unemployment are often overqualified, underutilized, or hired at lower compensation levels because it is a buyer's market. Further, in rapidly growing, emerging markets, the abundance of low-skilled workers often means a booming economy built on the backs of laborers in modern-day sweatshops and factories, sometimes with disastrous workplace tragedies. In hotter job markets (which have tighter talent pools), many employees choose to jump from one job to another in order to quickly move up the title and salary ladder, developing little commitment to a company, its customers, or its mission.

Against that backdrop, it's hard to believe that any company has the kind of employee population that can make it successful, given the challenging economies, increasing pressures from new competitors, rising pace of technological change, increasing government regulation, and heightened geopolitical risk. Yet there are still companies who outperform their industry peers, even when so many of their products, services, structures, and challenges are surprisingly similar. These high-performing companies excel at a variety of business metrics, from shareholder value to operating margin to workplace safety. They are more likely to be innovative. They have stronger employee value propositions to retain key employees and a compelling brand to attract new talent.

What makes this critical difference? Many would argue that the difference is an engaged workforce that consistently delivers superior performance, creates innovative products and solutions, and serves as a brand ambassador to drive customer loyalty and attract great candidates.

So, what can companies do to stem the tide of worker malaise and distrust? How can they drive high levels of employee engagement, or build a culture of engagement that fosters the kind of employee performance that makes the difference between survival and success? And even more important, how do they measure the impact so that they know whether they are successful? The answer is to develop employee engagement programs and initiatives at the organizational or business unit level. This begins with an examination of the macro level of employee engagement: what employee engagement is, the factors that drive (or hinder) engaged workforces, the evolution of the concept of engagement, the state of engagement and engagement practices today, and thoughts on building a culture of engagement.

The Drivers of Engagement

There is a great deal of research about what actually drives engagement, which usually reflects aspects of the business culture, relationships with supervisors, and workload. Well-known assessments by Towers Watson, U.S. Merit Systems Protection Board, and The Conference Board have revealed many insights about employee engagement (Ray 2011).

Towers Watson's *2014 Global Workforce Study* lists five global top drivers of sustainable engagement that focus on behaviors and actions that matter to employees:

- leadership: is effective at growing the business; earns employee's trust and confidence; behaves consistently with the organization's core values; envisions the future; inspires others to follow; transforms the organization to achieve the vision; and adapts to changing internal and external conditions
- organization's image: highly regarded by general public; displays honesty and integrity in business activities
- goals and objectives: employees understand the organization's business goals, steps they need to take to reach those goals, have the resources and support to do the job effectively, and see how their job contributes to achieving goals
- work/life balance: manageable levels of stress at work; a work environment that supports well-being, a healthy balance between work and personal life, and provides flexible work arrangements

- communications: managers act in ways consistent with their words, treat employees with respect, clearly communicate goals and assignments, help remove obstacles to success, and coach employees to improve performance.

The Merit Principles Survey, which is administered to more than 36,000 workers by the U.S. Merit Systems Protection Board, asks questions to elicit information about these drivers:

- pride in one's work or workplace
- satisfaction with leadership
- opportunity to perform well at work
- satisfaction with recognition received
- prospect for future personal and professional growth
- a positive work environment with some focus on teamwork.

Research from The Conference Board revealed these eight drivers of engagement to be key:

- trust and integrity
- nature of the job
- line of sight between individual performance and company performance
- career growth opportunities
- pride about the company
- co-workers and team members
- employee development
- personal relationship with one's manager.

Drivers of engagement have been relatively consistent over time; however, recognition and the desire to do meaningful work (aligning with the mission of the organization) are both being mentioned as contributors to employee engagement more frequently now than in the past.

STAGES OF ENGAGEMENT

Engagement science has been evolving for some time, and it has already had a major impact on organizations in terms of what they do and their success. But there is a lot of potential for the future. It is helpful to review the status of engagement through the stages of its development—the research pinpointing how it arrived and morphed into a powerful topic, its status as a process and a practice, and its impact.

Research

From its origins as research about "employee motivation" in the mid-1950s, predominantly among companies in the United States, to "job satisfaction," "employee commitment," and finally "employee engagement," these employee engagement attempts have sought to link worker attitudes to productivity with the belief (even in the absence of definitive proof) that engaged workers are more productive and valuable than those who are not.

Management theory, including the early work of Mary Parker Follett in the 1920s, has long sought to understand the ways in which organizational structure and management practice can affect employee behavior, resulting in improved business performance. In the 1950s and 1960s, researchers such as Frederick Herzberg studied employee motivation and the elements of the workplace that drove either satisfaction or dissatisfaction, concluding that these elements are often very different things (Herzberg 2003). Perhaps the most important pioneer in terms of engagement is Scott Myers, who integrated the research of many people, including Rensis Likert, Douglas McGregor, David McClelland, Abraham Maslow, Chris Argyris, and Frederick Herzberg. Combining all this research and making sense of it in terms of its implications for employees and their work, Myers published a book in 1970 to name and explain the concept he developed: *Every Employee a Manager*. In this work, Myers showed how all employees can and should manage their work to a certain extent, with some obvious limitations. He argued that jobs can mostly be managed by individuals, which then allows them to feel ownership and responsibility for their work; it's the ultimate form of engagement. Myers was able to make this theory understandable and put it into practice, and he worked with many executives to bring this concept to job design and supervisory practices, as well as human resources programs.

Job satisfaction surveys elicit information about the way employees feel about their work environment, compensation, company benefits, and management, among other aspects of their workplace. Examinations of the concept of job satisfaction began to appear in the academic literature in the mid-1960s, notably *The Measure of Satisfaction in Work and Retirement: A Strategy for the Study of Attitudes* (Smith, Kendall, and Hulin 1969).

Rates of job satisfaction in the United States have suffered for a variety of reasons, including the erosion of employee loyalty in the 1980s, when pension plans changed and offshore hiring, layoffs, and plant closures shattered what had become an employee expectation of stable, long-term employment. As part of one of the longest-running examinations of job satisfaction in the United States, The Conference Board's 2013 study revealed that less than half (47.3 percent) of U.S. workers are satisfied with their jobs, compared to the 61.1 percent in 1987, the first year of analysis. This reflects a steady decline in job satisfaction over the decades, which hit its lowest point in 2010 at 42.6 percent and has only recently returned to pre–Great Recession levels (Ray, Levanon, and Rizzacasa 2013). However, while these concepts are related, job satisfaction is not the same as engagement.

Academic research specifically regarding employee engagement began to appear in the early 1990s. Even then, research posited that engaged and disengaged workers offer varying degrees of "effort" and are, at various times, more or less committed to the work and the workplace, as explained in "Psychological Conditions of Personal Engagement and Disengagement at Work" (Kahn 1990). This more esoteric academic work continued to explore the ways in which employees feel (or fail to feel) connected to the workplace.

The 2002 *Journal of Applied Psychology* article "Business-Unit-Level Relationship Between Employee Satisfaction, Employee Engagement, and Business Outcomes: A Meta-Analysis" was among the first attempts to quantify engagement in terms of business results. Business leaders finally took notice, causing a dramatic shift in the level of attention paid to, and investments in, employee engagement (Harter, Schmidt, and Hayes 2002).

Practice

Despite all the energy, effort, and resources devoted to the issue of employee engagement, overall engagement levels in the workforce remain low and largely unchanged. The 2013 Gallup report *The State of the Global Workplace* revealed that only 13 percent of workers are engaged, 63 percent are not engaged, and 24 percent are actively disengaged. Globally, workers in East Asia (largely China) were among the least engaged, at 6 percent, whereas 24 percent of workers in New Zealand and Australia were engaged and only 16 percent are actively disengaged. The highest levels of active disengagement in the world (35 percent) can be found in the Middle East and North Africa (Gallup 2013b). In the United States, among its nearly 1 million full-time employees, 30 percent are engaged, 50 percent are not engaged, and 20 percent are actively disengaged (Gallup 2013a).

Engagement rates differ by age, occupation, gender, seniority level, remote versus on-site location, educational level, region, country, and state. When organizations can determine levels of engagement on a granular level (for example, business unit or division, or employee population or team leader) then a clearer picture emerges as to the relative performance of the groups against their peers. It is only when those data becomes actionable for the short term or even predictive for the long term that employee engagement data have any real value.

Among the most common issues that surface in employee engagement surveys are poor management and leadership, a lack of career opportunities, limited professional growth, a disconnect from the mission or strategy of the organization, a negative perception of the organization's future, and an unmanageable workload. In 2012, The Conference Board surveyed engagement leaders at 209 companies in 21 countries to determine, among other things, what engagement practices, programs, and initiatives are most prevalent (Ray, Powers, and Stathatos 2012). According to the report *Employee Engagement—What Works Now?* the engagement function reports to the chief human resources officer 52 percent of the time and to another senior HR executive 27 percent of the time, making this clearly a process still owned by human resources. In addition, of those surveyed:

- 89 percent said they have an engagement strategy in place.
- 52 percent report that their organizations have been focused on engagement for more than five years.
- 41 percent administer an annual engagement survey and 27 percent administer one biannually, while 25 percent survey more frequently and 7 percent do not survey at all.
- 84 percent indicated that their company's approach to employee engagement strategy has changed in the last six to 24 months, either greatly (26 percent) or somewhat (58 percent), with many indicating that the change was a matter of "more focus" on engagement or increased accountability.
- 49 percent work for organizations that link employee performance and results to engagement.

Despite the importance of engagement, 48 percent of those surveyed said that no one was dedicated full time to engagement activities, and another 29 percent indicated they had only one to three full-time employees dedicated to administering, monitoring, and analyzing these programs.

Value

Employee engagement is critical to business performance and a success factor on many levels, from executing business strategy to financial performance to worker productivity to the ability to create innovative products and services. According to the *Conference Board CEO Challenge 2014*—in which more than 1,000 CEOs, presidents, and chairpeople listed their most critical areas of concern for the coming year as well as the strategies they plan to use to address these challenges—human capital issues are a top challenge globally, ranking first or second in every region, including China and India (Mitchell, Ray, and van Ark 2014).

Continuing its steady rise in the ranking of strategies to address the human capital challenge, "raise employee engagement" ranked second in 2014, up from third in the 2013 survey and eighth in the 2012 survey. In addition, respondents indicated the critical linkage between "human capital" and their next four challenges: "customer relationships," "innovation," "operational excellence," and "corporate brand and reputation." In fact, engagement is also a top-five strategy to address the challenges of innovation and operational excellence. Respondents in this survey have clearly put employees at the center of everything.

One of the most comprehensive studies showing the business impact of employee engagement, *The Relationship Between Engagement at Work and Organizational Outcomes*, reveals that engagement is indeed related to the nine performance outcomes selected for the study—customer loyalty and engagement, profitability, productivity, turnover, safety incidents, shrinkage, absenteeism, patient safety incidents, and quality (defects)—with consistent correlations across organizations (Harter, Schmidt, Agrawal, and Plowman 2013). The study also found that:

- Business and work units scoring in the top half on employee engagement nearly double their odds of success compared with those in the bottom half.
- Those in the 99th percentile have four times the success rate as those in the first percentile.
- Median differences between top-quartile and bottom-quartile employee engagement units were 10 percent in customer ratings, 22 percent in profitability, 21 percent in productivity, 25 and 65 percent in turnover (for high- and low-turnover organizations, respectively), 48 percent in safety incidents, 28 percent in shrinkage (theft), 37 percent in absenteeism, 41 percent in patient safety incidents, and 41 percent in quality (defects).

Employee Engagement and Earnings per Share: A Longitudinal Study of Organizational Performance During the Recession, reveals a correlation between earnings per share and employee engagement levels finding that those organizations with the most engaged workers exceeded the earnings per share (EPS) of their competition (even widening their lead during the recession) by 72 percent (Harter, Agrawal, Plowman, and Asplund 2010).

These findings are underscored in Gallup's latest *State of the Global Workplace,* which states that engaged employees worldwide are twice as likely to report that their organizations are hiring (versus disengaged employees) and that "organizations with an average of 9.3 engaged workers for every actively disengaged employee in 2010-2011 experienced 147 percent higher EPS compared with their competition in 2011-2012. In contrast, those with an average of 2.6 engaged employees for every actively disengaged employee experienced 2 percent lower EPS compared with their competition during the same period" (Gallup 2013b).

The linkage between employee engagement and business metrics can also be found in Towers Watson's *2012 Global Workforce Study,* which found that higher levels of engagement can translate into higher operating margins—from just below 10 percent for companies with low traditional engagement levels to just over 14 percent for those with high traditional engagement to more than 27 percent for those with high sustainable engagement. These engagement levels were defined by the intensity of employees' connection to their organization based on three core elements: being engaged, feeling enabled, and feeling energized.

The study also found that highly engaged workers have lower rates of presenteeism (lost productivity at work; 7.6 days per year versus 14.1 days per year) and absenteeism (3.2 days per year versus 4.2 days per year) than disengaged workers. They are also less likely to report an intention to leave their employers within the next two years versus the highly disengaged (18 percent and 40 percent, respectively), and 72 percent would prefer to remain with their employers even if offered a comparable position elsewhere.

Great Place to Work, a consulting and research firm, has studied engagement in the workplace for decades and includes trust as part of its model. Companies selected for inclusion on the "Great Places to Work" list, in partnership with *Fortune* magazine, exhibit a higher degree of trust and engagement in the workplace than other companies. The organization has found that committed and engaged employees who trust their management perform 20 percent better and are 87 percent less likely to leave an organization, resulting in easier employee and management recruitment, decreased training costs, and incalculable value in retained tenure equity. In addition, analysts indicate that publicly traded companies on the "100 Best Companies to Work For" list consistently outperform major stock indices by 300 percent and have half the voluntary turnover rates of their competitors.

We live in an age where maintaining an organization's reputation and brand is a constant challenge, especially as organizations seek to retain current customers and attract new ones. Frontline employees are the key to success with customers. Numerous studies point to the importance of employee engagement on customer satisfaction— research indicates that the customers of engaged employees use their products more, which leads to higher levels of customer satisfaction, and that these employees influence the behavior and attitudes of their customers, which drives profitability (Ray 2011). Engagement (or lack thereof) can also be measured in terms of economic impact with wide-ranging implications for countries and regions. While few employees are engaged and many more are not engaged, companies would do well to take action to mitigate the impact of the actively disengaged. Gallup estimates that economic loss from active disengagement costs the United States between $450 and $550 billion per year. In Germany, that figure ranges from €112 to €138 billion per year (US$151 to $186 billion). In the United Kingdom, actively disengaged employees cost the country between £52 and £70 billion (US$83 billion and $112 billion) per year (Gallup 2013b). In addition to determining the impact on business performance, human capital programs and initiatives also rely on employee engagement data. According to a report by Bersin, 57 percent of HR practitioners indicated that the employee engagement metric was their most important in terms of determining talent management success (Harris 2010).

MACRO VERSUS MICRO VIEW

When executives suggest that engagement is at the top of their list, they are placing a value on engagement based on their logical view of the process: If employees are more engaged, they are probably producing more, are more safety conscious, enjoy their work, and will stay with the organization. Because executives want their employees to be engaged, they are willing to invest in this important area and support it.

However, the logical view is not always enough. Practitioners may need to demonstrate the macro view of employee engagement across an organization. This view—comprising studies that connect engagement with many different outcomes—is important, especially when convincing executives who are faced with trying to understand the value of employee engagement.

Yet, even this still may not be enough. Executives may want to see studies that indicate the value of engagement in their organization. If they are investing X amount in employee engagement, what is the monetary benefit derived? They need to see the actual ROI. Just because studies show that more engagement among employees drives productivity, it doesn't mean that executives will take the need for engagement for granted. They may want to know, "But what about my organization?" To answer that question, studies are needed at the organizational level showing the value of engagement, converting the value of engagement to monetary benefits, and comparing that with the investment in engagement to show the ROI. This represents the micro analysis. Fortunately, this book shows how this actually done.

A MODEL FOR ENGAGEMENT IMPLEMENTATION

It is helpful to understand engagement from the perspective of how it is introduced and implemented in an organization. The implementation usually follows several prescribed steps, and there are many different approaches offered in terms of how engagement is delivered. Exhibit 1-2 shows a nine-step engagement model that brings engagement into the organization with a constant focus on the business contribution of the engagement process. As with most important processes, engagement starts with alignment to the business in the beginning and ends with measuring the impact on the business in a very logical, rational way. The model is presented in a cyclical fashion because engagement is a never-ending adjustment process—practitioners should always be collecting data to see how things are working and making adjustments when they are not. The next nine sections provide more detail on this model.

Align Employee Engagement to the Business

The beginning point with any process is alignment to the business, and engagement should be no different. Determining business needs and business value is the beginning point that executives want to see. This is expressed through classic measures in the system, usually reflecting output, quality, cost, and time. These critical data are reported throughout the system in scorecards, dashboards, key performance indicators, operating reports, and many other vehicles. A new HR program or employee engagement initiative should begin with the end in mind, focusing on one business measure (such as productivity, sales, customer satisfaction, employee retention, quality, or cycle times).

Exhibit 1-2. Engagement Model

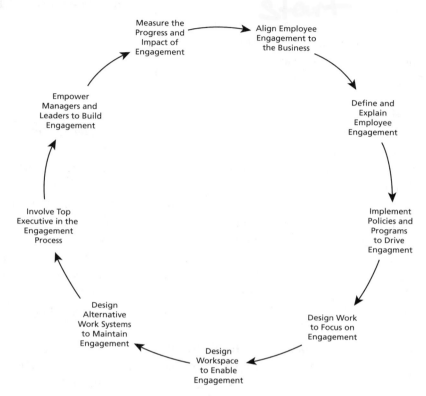

The challenge is to identify which measures should change if employees are more actively engaged. The literature is full of hypotheses on these issues, all claiming a variety of results. This quick review can help management understand what might come out of the program. The important point is that if a measure is identified, it is more likely that the engagement process will actually achieve its goal. Beginning with the end in mind is the best driver for the outcomes of the process.

Employee engagement scores, taken either annually or biannually, are impact data, because they indicate the collective impact of all the engagement processes in the organization. These data only describe perceptions, but they are still very important. Engagement on its own is an intangible measure in the scheme of impact measures. Unfortunately, many organizations early in the process stop there, merely reporting improvements in engagement scores. This leads many executives to respond, "So what?"

Thus, practitioners have to do more, and doing more means that the results of engagement must be identified at the macro and micro levels. The business impact is the linkage of engagement with certain outcome measures in the business category.

The efforts of the HR team should be to illustrate the significant correlation and causation between improvements in engagement scores and outcome measures, which can typically be expressed in statements such as:

- Engagement drives productivity.
- Engagement drives quality.
- Engagement drives sales.
- Engagement drives retention.
- Engagement drives safety.

Others have developed more specific measures to link to engagement, such as processing times for loans to be underwritten, purchase cost for the procurement function, or security breaches in the IT function. In other words, engagement scores can be linked to many outcomes, and the HR function's challenge is to show that.

Another way to show the business value of engagement is to connect it to individual projects. In this case, it is not just the overall engagement score that is linked to the business measures from a macro prospective but also an individual project involving individual participants. For example, a manufacturing plant used job engagement to improve quality of work. The study tracking the success of the program examined the improvements in quality, converted them to a monetary value, and then compared that with the cost of the program to yield a ROI of 399 percent (Phillips and Phillips 2012).

Define and Explain Employee Engagement

While there are many definitions of employee engagement, they are remarkably similar in their emphasis on several common elements. The following come from a review of engagement definitions found in *Employee Engagement in a V.U.C.A. World* (Ray 2011):

- According to The Conference Board, "Employee engagement is a heightened emotional and intellectual connection that an employee has for his/her job, organization, manager, or coworkers that, in turn, influences him/her to apply additional discretionary effort to his/her work."
- Towers Watson delineated employee engagement along three dimensions:
  - Rational: How well employees understand their roles and responsibilities.
  - Emotional: How much passion employees bring to the work and their organizations
  - Motivational: How willing employees are to invest discretionary effort to perform roles well.
- The U.S. Merit Systems Protection Board states, "Employee engagement is a heightened connection between employees and their work, their organization, or the people they work for or with."
- According to Korn Ferry, "Employee engagement is a mindset in which employees take personal stakeholder responsibility for the success of the organization and apply discretionary efforts aligned with its goals."

These definitions suggest alignment with the organization and a willingness to expend discretionary effort as critical components of employee engagement. Further, the Gallup Organization (2013a) delineates three types of employees:

- Engaged employees work with passion and feel a profound connection to their company. They drive innovation and move the organization forward.
- Not-engaged employees are essentially "checked out." They're sleepwalking through the workday, putting time—but not energy or passion—into their work.
- Actively disengaged employees aren't just unhappy at work; they're busy acting out their unhappiness. Every day, these workers undermine what their engaged co-workers accomplish.

Of note, one of the more recent developments in this space has been a focus on well-being, which links engagement to health issues as part of a movement toward holistic work environments. Another development is a focus on happiness, which seeks a holistic approach to worker contentment by weighing two components: overall life satisfaction and affect balance. (For an overview of this concept as well as profiles of examinations of happiness at Zappos, Google, HCL, Best Buy, and Southwest Airlines, see *The Happiness Premium: What Companies Should Know About Leveraging Happiness in the Workplace*.)

Executives must communicate not only what engagement means, but how it affects them and how their role will change. This part of this step in the model is critical, because it connects the executives to the process and fully explains what is involved. Some of this may involve stories that are told about what it means to be engaged. For example, there is the classic story of the janitor at NASA who was asked, "What is your job?" while he was sweeping the floors. He answered that he was helping put a man on the moon. Although this may appear to be an odd example, it is the kind of thinking and attitude that is sought through the engagement process. Stories, memos, meetings, speeches, and even formal documents can help define and explain the goal of the process.

Implement Policies and Programs to Drive Engagement

The next part of the process is to enact the different formal processes that address the engagement issue. The starting point is showing the mission, vision, and values of the organization. These are well-documented in most organizations, but the key is to integrate some language around engagement. For example, here is what Tony Hsieh, CEO of Zappos.com, says about engagement:

> We have 10 core values, and when we hire people, we make sure they have similar values. For example, one of our values is to be humble. If someone comes in and is really egotistical, even if they are the greatest, most talented person technically and we know they could do a lot for our top or bottom line, we won't hire them, because they are not a culture fit. (Reiss 2010)

15

After engagement is clearly defined and the dimensions of work that connect with the definition are clearly described, a survey is usually developed that secures the perception from employees. This initial survey is designed to reveal the current status of engagement, and the resulting data are used to make improvements. This is a classic survey-feedback-action loop that many organizations use as they survey employees, provide feedback to the survey respondents, and plan actions during the year to improve engagement. It is not only a routine, formal practice; it becomes the principal process improvement tool as changes and adjustments are made each year based on the engagement survey results.

Engagement is usually a principal component or determinate of a great place to work. For example, in *Fortune's* "100 Best Companies to Work For," two-thirds of the determinate for being on the list is the score of an engagement survey given to a randomly selected sample of employees. These are very powerful data, and a positive score is desired by the executive team. Being included on such a list helps attract and retain employees, and although the award itself is intangible, it is connected to tangible measures.

Among HR functions, specific adjustments can be made to improve various components of engagement. For example, recruiting and selection processes can include letting potential audiences know about the organization's efforts to have employees fully engaged. Selection may be based on the desire of employees to be engaged in the organization, and more emphasis may be given to onboarding as a process of aligning people with the philosophy of the organization.

The company can also develop training and learning programs to reinforce the principles of engagement; even the method of learning is sometimes adjusted to be more adaptive to the individuals in organizations. Ideally, training is perceived as just in time, just enough, and just for me. It is customized for individuals and provided at the time they need it.

Compensation can be adjusted to reward individuals for being more engaged. Engagement often leads to improved financial outcomes, which sometimes means paying for bonuses, as is particularly true for salespeople. It also can be expanded into general recognition programs where individuals are rewarded for displaying proper engagement behaviors or managers and supervisors are rewarded for reinforcing them. In essence, any HR function that involves employees and influences employee behavior can have an important impact on engagement.

Design Work to Focus on Engagement

A huge part of this process is to make sure that the work inherently allows for engagement—for thinking and being empowered. It can be very frustrating for employees when they are asked to be more engaged but are still constrained by old job descriptions and structures.

Sometimes it is helpful to think about "where the work comes from." Before work can be done, there are management functions that must be fulfilled:

- planning: objectives, goals, strategies, programs, systems, policies, forecasts
- organizing: staffing, budgets, equipment, materials, methods
- leading: communicating, motivating, facilitating, delegating, mediating, counseling
- controlling: auditing, measuring, evaluating, correcting.

Traditionally, these functions are all centralized in a manager, supervisor, or designated leader, and work is prescribed for employees exactly, sometimes allowing no deviation from their job descriptions. But with an engagement perspective, employees are expected to get more involved in planning what work to do, when to do it, how goals and standards can be met, and maybe even how to source the information or materials needed. They may be involved in not only doing the job but controlling it, verifying the quality of the product, checking to see how procedures are working, making adjustments, and so forth.

This concept of empowerment is a vital part of engagement. Empowered employees take initiative and are held responsible for the things they do. They have ownership in the process, and thus they become fully engaged. Empowerment programs have been implemented for some time and are an important part of driving the engagement process.

Design Workspaces to Enable Engagement

The workspaces of organizations have changed dramatically—from private offices and cubicles to rotating desk assignments, couches, standing desks, treadmill desks, and even no desks. One constant thing in the process is that offices have become more open. In fact, this openness has been evolving for many years. According to the International Facility Management Association, today more than 70 percent of employees work in an open-space environment, and the size of the workplace has shrunk from 225 square feet per employee in 2010 to 190 square feet in 2013. In short, workplaces are smaller and more open, which leads to some concerns.

One concern is the actual size of the office. Does it still provide enough space? This is a concern for individuals who need a place for their accessories, devices, files, and work, which has led to some alternative configurations that provide a separate space, in addition to the actual workspace. Another concern is privacy. Privacy issues have changed over the years as workplace design has evolved. According to Steelcase, one of the largest makers of office systems, there has been a shifting need for privacy. In the 1980s there was a call for more privacy and less interaction, but by the 1990s offices were built with less privacy and more interaction. Now the pendulum is swinging back in the other direction, and there is a call for more privacy, but more interaction through interactive devices (Congdon, Flynn, and Redman 2014). This leads to a concern for transparency because everyone now has access to everything that every-one else is doing. In an open office, employees can see computer screens, hear con-versations, read documents, and access all kinds of messages from different devices, making it perhaps too transparent for some. This is what is driving the swing to greater privacy.

Another concern is interruptions. Open offices invite people to interrupt fre-quently, as sometimes there is simply no door to shut. Managing interruptions can become a very difficult process. A similar concern is distraction. Hearing noises and seeing what is going on with other employees is a huge distraction to many people.

There are several major trends that have been occurring in workspace design. The first is to recognize the power of the open space environment, despite the concerns that arise from it. Exhibit 1-3 shows the relationship of space and performance (Waber, Magnolfi, and Lindsey 2014). Assigned cubicles and private offices are certainly good for individual performance, but they are not helpful for group productivity where there is a need for collaboration that leads to innovation. An innovative organization needs to be in the upper right-hand corner of the diagram, where offices are open and flex-ible and movement is possible between different offices, rooms, and activity areas. Collaboration is an important part of engagement, and it is also an important value for organizations trying to encourage high performance and innovation at the same time (CCIM Institute 1999).

Another important trend is that the space assigned to individuals should depend on the time that they spend in the office. If people only use their office a small part of the time, their office should be much smaller. This is a departure from the way in which office space was traditionally allocated: according to the title and rank of the employee. For example, executives who travel frequently may be given a small office because they are not there very often. On the other hand, workers involved in major projects may need the extra space.

Common areas are being developed to give people ample opportunities to have discussions. These areas can be walled off rooms, like conference rooms or meeting spaces at different places in an open environment, or simply little nooks for people to meet quickly, reflect, communicate with a small team, or otherwise pull people together.

Workspaces are being designed to get people to interact. For example, Samsung's new U.S. headquarters was designed in stark contrast to its traditional buildings. Vast outdoor public spaces are sandwiched between floors, a configuration that executives hope will lure engineers and salespeople into mingling. Likewise, Facebook's new office space puts several thousand of its employees, including the C-suite, into a single mile-long room. These companies know that a chance meeting with someone else in an office environment is a very important activity for collaboration.

Exhibit 1-3. Relationship of Space and Performance

	Private Offices	Open Offices
Flexible Seating	Individual and Small Group Creativity • Brainstorming • Small group creativity • Refinement	Group Innovation • No silos • Increased collaboration • More innovation
Assigned Seating	Individual Performance • Focused work	Group Performance • Project management • Group work

Adapted from Waber, Magnolfi, and Lindsey (2014).

A final trend is that workplaces are becoming more agile. They are not just for sitting anymore but also standing, walking, and moving. Research has shown that sitting at the computer all day is a very unhealthy practice, and many organizations are now trying to give employees the opportunity to get up often, move around, and in some cases even use a treadmill desk (Lohr 2012).

Design Alternative Work Systems to Maintain Engagement

In the last decade, much progress has been made with alternative work systems, particularly in allowing employees to work from home. In this arrangement, actual employees (not contractors) perform work for their organization at home for a set number of days each week. This enables a huge savings in real estate for the office, but there are many other benefits as well.

The arrangement that has perhaps the most impact is *working completely at home*. Employees essentially do all their work at home and very rarely make trips to the office, if at all. In this case, the home office is configured to be an efficient, safe, and healthy workplace. This requires effort on the part of the organization to ensure, from a technology perspective, that the employee functions the same way she would in the office.

Another arrangement is *office sharing,* where one or more employees share an office. In this case, they predominantly work at home, but spend short periods of time in the office. In an ideal situation, two people share one office, with the schedule arranged so that the two employees are not there at the same time.

A third option is *hoteling,* where several employees work at home but come into the office occasionally. A suite of offices is available, and they have to reserve the office space in advance to use it. Essentially, the office space functions as a hotel, where employees check in and out of workspaces.

A fourth type of work arrangement is *flextime,* where employees work at home and in the office, but set their own working hours as long as they work the prescribed number of hours. This often takes the form of a compressed work week, where employees work three days with longer hours and then have an extra two days off. It could also mean working slightly longer hours each day to have a half-day off, or coming to work early in the morning and leaving early in the afternoon.

Another option is *job sharing,* where two people are charged with doing one specific job. Each person works about half the hours, and they coordinate their schedules so that they are not both there at the same time. Essentially, they are teaming up to get the job done, but still working individually (each on a part-time basis).

Finally, there is *part-time work,* where individuals work reduced hours, receive limited benefits, and free up office space for others when they are not there. This allows employees the flexibility of having more time off while still remaining employed with the organization.

Whatever the arrangement, it has to be fully prescribed and have specific conditions and rules.

Involve Top Executives in the Engagement Process

The role of top executives is very critical in any process, but particularly with engagement. With so much evidence that engagement adds value and so much potential for it to add more, most executives are willing to step up and commit resources, time, and effort to make sure that engagement works. This involves several areas:

- **Commitment:** Executives should commit resources, staff, and other processes to make sure that engagement is properly developed, implemented, and supported in the organization.
- **Communication:** Employees carefully weigh messages from the senior executive team, and what the team says about the engagement process sets the tone for others. It also shows the position of executives. Top executives should be involved in major announcements, the rollout of programs, progress assessments, and any major actions taken as a result of engagement input.

- **Involvement:** Top executives must be involved in these programs. They should kick off programs and moderate town-hall meetings about engagement. They should participate in learning programs on preparing leaders and managers to build engagement in the organization.
- **Recognition:** Top executives have to recognize those who are doing the best job. The best way to recognize exemplars of engagement is to promote them, reward them, and publicly recognize them. Engagement data should be placed alongside key operating results for this to be effective.
- **Support:** Support is more than just providing resources and recognizing those who achieve results; it also means supporting the programs and encouraging people to be involved and take action. This shows that leaders genuinely support these programs and their success.
- **Long-Term Thinking:** Engagement cannot be seen as a fad that comes through the organization only to be abandoned for the next one. Too often this occurs in organizations—executives work on "engagement" this year, "lean thinking" the next year, and "open-book management" the year after that. The key is to stay with it and make it work.
- **Reference:** Refer to engagement often as a driver of gross productivity, sales, and profits. Making reference to engagement regularly in meetings, reports, press releases, and annual shareholder meetings brings the importance of the process into focus. Collectively, these efforts from top executives, which are often coordinated by the chief human resources officer, will make a difference in the success of the engagement effort.

Empower Managers and Leaders to Build Engagement

First-level managers are key in the organization. They are in the position to make or break engagement, and they have to be prepared for it. The first step is to conduct learning programs where the issue of engagement is discussed—how they can encourage it, support it, and build it in their work teams. This provides awareness of engagement and skill-building around the components of engagement to make the process successful in the organization.

Most important, first-level managers must understand why engagement makes a difference. They must become role models of engagement and take an active part in ensuring that employees are empowered, involved in key decisions, and assume ownership and accountability for what they do. Managers must demonstrate what has to be done to make the engagement process work, and they must genuinely support it. They must reinforce the concept of engagement, what it means to them, and their roles in the process.

Much of this involves learning—learning what engagement is about and what makes it work but also what it can do for the organization. Position engagement as a process similar to sales training for a sales team or production training for the production group. It is an important process that managers must learn, apply, and use to drive results. This also means that they have to redefine success—success is not just knowing something, but making it work and having an impact. Making it work involves the behaviors that are exhibited as people collaborate to complete projects, but the impact must show up in improved measures of productivity, innovation, quality, and efficiency.

First-level managers are critical, because they must use all the tools generated around engagement. The HR team offers the many processes and tools to be implemented, but the frontline leaders make the difference by using the tools appropriately, following up to make sure they work, and reporting issues and concerns back to the HR team.

Measure the Progress and Impact of Engagement

Measurement for this process involves several issues. The first is measuring the progress with engagement through an annual survey. This assesses the perceptions employees have about the progress they are making. The annual survey must include several major elements to make it successful:

- It must be carefully planned, perhaps including input from those who are being assessed.
- The data must be collected anonymously or confidentially. This is a time to collect candid feedback on the progress being made.
- The data must be reported back to the respondents quickly, so that they can see what the group has said locally and globally.
- There must be follow-up, immediately and later—all in reference to the engagement program. This survey-feedback-action loop will ensure that the process is taken seriously.

Another measurement issue is linking the engagement scores to a variety of outcome measures such as productivity, sales, retention, quality, and safety. It is a way for the organization, executives, and HR team to see the value of this process.

Success should also be measured in terms of individual projects, such as communications, coaching, team building, management development, and leadership development. These are all programs that involve parts of the engagement process. It is helpful to connect particular programs not only to engagement but also to individual measures that may improve in this process.

Finally, measuring ROI is the mandate for many top executives. If the engagement team can show executives the return on investing in engagement, it reinforces their commitment to make the process work, and it often improves their relationship with those involved in engagement, as well as their respect for the entire talent management and human resources function. Pushing at least some of the programs to the ROI level is very helpful, and ultimately it is possible to show the ROI of the entire engagement process.

FINAL THOUGHTS

This opening chapter explored a variety of issues that surround employee engagement and set the stage for how to measure the success of employee engagement programs. The strategic importance of engagement was discussed, the stages of engagement were examined, and a model for successfully implementing an engagement program was presented. As with most important processes, engagement starts with alignment to the business in the beginning and ends with measuring the impact on the business in a logical, rational way. The next six chapters outline the necessary, relevant steps to using the ROI Methodology with employee engagement to clearly show the impact and ROI of these important programs.

REFERENCES

CCIM Institute. 1999. "Ten Trends in Office Design." *CIRE Magazine,* March-April. www.ccim.com/cire-magazine/articles/10-trends-office-design.

Congdon, C., D. Flynn, and M. Redman. 2014. "Balancing We and Me." *Harvard Business Review,* October.

Gallup. 2013a. *State of the American Workplace: Employee Engagement Insights for U.S. Business Leaders.* www.gallup.com/services/178514/state-american-workplace .aspx.

Gallup. 2013b. *State of the Global Workplace: Employee Engagement Insights for Business Leaders Worldwide.* www.gallup.com/services/178517/state-global-workplace .aspx.

Harris, S. 2010. *Measuring the Business Impact of Talent Strategies.* Bersin & Associates.

Harter, J., S. Agrawal, S. Plowman, and J. Asplund. 2010. *Employee Engagement and Earnings per Share: A Longitudinal Study of Organizational Performance During the Recession.* Gallup.

Harter, J.K., F.L. Schmidt, S. Agrawal, and S.K. Plowman. 2013. *The Relationship Between Engagement at Work and Organizational Outcomes.* Gallup. www.gallup .com/services/177047/q12-meta-analysis.aspx.

Harter, K., F.L. Schmidt, and T.L. Hayes. 2002. "Business-Unit-Level Relationship Between Employee Satisfaction, Employee Engagement, and Business Outcomes: A Meta-Analysis." *Journal of Applied Psychology* 87:268-279.

Herzberg, F. 2003. "One More Time: How Do You Motivate Employees?" *Harvard Business Review,* January.

International Facility Management Association (IFMA). 2010. *Space and Project Management Benchmarks IFMA Research Report #34.* Houston: IFMA.

Kahn, W.A. 1990. "Psychological Conditions of Personal Engagement and Disengagement at Work." *The Academy of Management Journal* 33(4): 692-724.

Lohr, S. 2012. "Taking a Stand for Office Ergonomics." *New York Times*, December 1.

Mitchell, C., R. Ray, and B. van Ark. 2014. *The Conference Board CEO Challenge 2014: People and Performance*. New York: The Conference Board.

Morgan, J. 2014. *The Future of Work: Attract New Talent, Build Better Leaders, and Create a Competitive Organization*. Hoboken, NJ: Wiley.

Myers, M.S. 1970. *Every Employee a Manager: More Meaningful Work Through Job Enrichment*. New York: McGraw-Hill.

Nayar, V. 2010. *Employees First, Customers Second: Turning Conventional Management Upside Down*. Boston: Harvard Business School Press.

Phillips, P.P., and J.J. Phillips. 2014. *Measuring ROI in Employee Relations and Compliance: Case Studies in Diversity and Inclusion, Engagement, Compliance and Flexible Working Arrangements*. Alexandria, VA: Society for Human Resource Management.

Phillips, P.P., and J.J. Phillips. 2012. *Measuring ROI in Learning and Development: Case Studies From Global Organizations*. Alexandria, VA: ASTD Press.

Phillips, P.P., J.J. Phillips, and R. Ray. 2015. *Measuring the Success of Leadership Development: A Step-by-Step Guide for Measuring Impact and Calculating ROI*. Alexandria, VA: ATD Press.

Ray, R., B. Powers, and P. Stathatos. 2012. *Employee Engagement: What Works Now?* New York: The Conference Board.

Ray, R., G. Levanon, and T. Rizzacasa. 2013. *Job Satisfaction 2013 Edition: At Least We're Working; Maybe That's Enough*. New York: The Conference Board.

Ray, R. 2011. *Employee Engagement in a V.U.C.A. World*. New York: The Conference Board.

Reiss, R. 2010. "Tony Hsieh on His Secrets of Success." *Forbes*, July 1. www.forbes.com/2010/07/01/tony-hsiesh-zappos-leadership-managing-interview.html.

Rizzacasa, T., and S. Nair. 2013. *The Happiness Premium: What Companies Should Know About Leveraging Happiness in the Workplace*. Executive action report. New York: The Conference Board.

Smith, P.C., L.M. Kendall, and C.L. Hulin. 1969. *The Measure of Satisfaction in Work and Retirement: A Strategy for the Study of Attitudes*. Chicago: Rand McNally Psychology Series.

Towers Watson. 2014. *2014 Global Workforce Study.* www.towerswatson.com/en-US
/Insights/IC-Types/Survey-Research-Results/2014/08/the-2014-global-workforce
-study.

Towers Watson. 2012. *2012 Global Workforce Study.* www.towerswatson.com/Insights
/IC-Types/Survey-Research-Results/2012/07/2012-Towers-Watson-Global-Workforce
-Study.

Waber, B., J. Magnolfi, and G. Lindsey. 2014. "Work Spaces That Move People."
Harvard Business Review, October.

2

A System for Measuring the Impact and ROI

While employee engagement is increasingly observed as a critical factor in organizations, the implications of measurement are also significant. To build a measurement process, certain steps need to be taken. It is in this context that the ROI Methodology is presented. In this chapter, we address using the ROI Methodology with engagement and how engagement teams are a conduit of change in building a measurement system.

HOW AND WHY ENGAGEMENT FITS WITH ROI

Engagement practitioners tend to be more socially driven (to help others) rather than financially driven. So what would drive an engagement practitioner to pursue ROI? Perhaps this is best answered by considering how and why ROI helps the process, and ultimately the client, by showing how the engagement has yielded the desired change.

The Engagement Practitioner as a Change Agent

Practitioners often view their role as one who influences an individual, group, or organization to a more desired change. The change agent plays a significant role in leading the change effort or collaborating with the team assigned to initiating change. Trying to create an environment that is measurement friendly also involves a change agent—someone to lead this effort and manage the change process within an organization.

It is important to remember that building a measurement system should be a strategic change. The change agent must set the stage with the "why" behind building a measurement culture, make sure that the change effort is in sync with what's important for the organization, and include action planning and feedback to keep the momentum building. It is also helpful to involve people who are senior in the organization because they have the clout necessary to pave the way for building a measurement system.

Identify a System to Routinely Review Measures

Adopting a systematic way to plan, collect, analyze, and report on programs in the organization, such as the ROI Methodology, begins the process of communicating and reinforcing what is important to the organization, while sending a clear message to key stakeholders as to what needs to change to improve outcomes. This is particularly true when measurement has been planned in advance to collect data points that tell the story in a comprehensive way. Exhibit 2-1 shows a clear delineation between activity-based and results-based initiatives. The old "if you build it, they will come" mentality can be challenged through a series of filtering questions:

- Is this initiative aligned with business impact or organization effectiveness outcomes?
- Is there an assessment of performance that shows a gap in performance?
- Is the work environment prepared to reinforce the implementation of engagement?
- Have partnerships been established with key stakeholders to support this initiative?
- Are there specific, measurable objectives for expected behavior change and business impact?

When employee engagement programs are aligned with results-based initiatives or what's important to the organization, it becomes more likely that engagement programs are easily measured and supported. The old adage rings true in this context: What gets measured gets done.

Exhibit 2-1. Activity-Based Versus Results-Based Approach to Engagement

Activity Based	Results Based
Business need is not linked to the employee engagement program in terms of monetary impact.	Initiative is linked to specific business impact or organizational effectiveness measures.
Assessment of performance issues that will be addressed in employee engagement program are not captured in a quantifiable, measureable manner.	There is a gap assessment of performance effectiveness that needs to be closed.
Specific, measurable, quantifiable objectives are not clarified.	Specific, measurable objectives for behavior change and the related business impact are identified.
Employees are not fully engaged or prepared to participate in the project.	Results expectations are communicated to, and in partnership with, employees.
The work environment is not prepared to reinforce the application or implementation of the employee engagement program to ensure behavior change and business impact.	The work environment is prepared to reinforce the application or implementation of the employee engagement program to ensure behavior change and business impact.

Activity Based	Results Based
Partnerships with key stakeholders to support the implementation have not been identified and developed.	Partnerships are established with key stakeholders prior to implementation to ensure participation and support.
Results or benefit-cost analysis in real, tangible, and objective measures—including monetary impact—are not captured.	Results and benefit-cost analysis are measured.
Planning and reporting is input focused.	Planning and reporting is outcome focused.

The ROI Methodology: A System for Accountability

The role of measurement and evaluation is crucial for establishing the impact and credibility of employee engagement. It is time for the field to fully accept its roots in a data-driven approach and understand the value inherent in measuring how and what we do. Several features about return on investment make it an effective measure for engagement:

- **To show bottom-line results for engagement.** Return on investment represents the ultimate range of measurement—a comparison of the actual cost of a project with its monetary benefits. This is done by using the same standard ratio that accountants have used for years to show the return on investment for a variety of investments, such as technology, equipment, and buildings.

- **Return on investment has a rich history of application.** The ROI Methodology is not a passing trend—it is a measure of accountability that has been in place for centuries. When resources are invested to address a business need, the ROI Methodology shows the financial impact of the investment.

- **To speak the same language as senior management.** Most managers have knowledge and skills for managing a business; some have degrees in business administration. These managers understand the need for a process to establish solid business cases and calculate a return on investment. They use ROI for a variety of projects and are fluid in carrying on conversations that measure the monetary results from large investments.

- **Return on investment generates a high degree of attention among key stakeholders.** Positive ROI outcomes create buzz and attention, particularly when the value exceeds expectations. Most stakeholders involved in engagement programs intuitively believe that the programs add value. But, they can use return on investment as a credible and valid measurement tool to confirm this hunch.

- **Using ROI Methodology forces the issue of strategic alignment.** By following the steps in the ROI process and conducting diagnostics with the multilevel framework for understanding business and performance needs, engagement will be more closely aligned with the strategic and operational needs of the business.

Gone are the days of indiscriminately increasing investment in human capital without any evidence regarding its impact on the business. When budget cuts are being made, human capital often rises to the top, and engagement projects are no exception.

These five factors are foundational for engagement practitioners to rethink the use of ROI Methodology and to implement this type of evaluation in specific projects. By using ROI Methodology, stakeholder groups will receive a comprehensive set of significant and balanced information about the success of an employee engagement initiative.

TYPES OF DATA FOR THE ROI METHODOLOGY

At the heart of the ROI Methodology is the variety of data that are collected throughout the process and reported at different intervals. Sometimes data are assigned a level because they reflect a successive effect in which one type of data affects the next. A number of tasks and fields use very logical steps of succession, and their use in a sequence can be linked to a variety of guidelines and models. The medical field, for example, uses levels in running and analyzing blood work. This not only helps the clinician understand the categories represented by the levels, it also helps the patient understand the results. The ROI Methodology is based on levels of evaluation, as shown in Exhibit 2-2.

As the evaluation moves to the higher levels, the value ascribed to the data by the client increases. Accordingly, the degree of effort and cost of capturing the data for the higher levels of evaluation also generally increase. With proper project planning and preparation, costs can be minimized.

Project Input Data

Level 0, inputs and indicators, represents a category of data that reveals the volume, time, and cost of employee engagement programs. It includes the number of people involved and the time of their involvement, representing a fully loaded cost profile. It reflects all direct and indirect costs. Level 0 data do not represent outcome data, but they are important because they represent the investment in engagement.

Exhibit 2-2. Six Categories of Data

Level	Measurement Focus	Typical Measures
0–Inputs and Indicators	Inputs into the employee engagement programs and processes including indicators representing scope, volumes, times, costs, and efficiencies	• Types of topics, content • Number of programs • Number of people • Hours of involvement • Costs
1–Reaction and Planned Action	Reaction to the engagement programs and processes including their perceived value	• Relevance • Importance • Usefulness • Appropriateness • Intent to use • Motivational • Recommended to others
2–Learning	Knowledge gained, learning how to develop concepts and how to become engaged at work	• Skills • Learning • Knowledge • Capacity • Competencies • Confidences • Contacts
3–Implementation	Application and use of engagement concepts in the work environment, including progress with implementation	• Behavior change • Extent of use • Task completion • Frequency of use • Actions completed • Success with use • Barriers to use • Enablers to use
4–Impact	The impact of the engagement programs and processes expressed as business impact and effectiveness measures	• Productivity • Revenue • Quality • Time • Efficiency • Accidents, incidents • Customer satisfaction • Employee engagement
5–ROI	Comparison of monetary benefits from the program with program costs	• Benefit-cost ratio (BCR) • ROI (%) • Payback period

Reaction Data

The first category of outcome data collected from a program is basic reaction data (Level 1 evaluation). This type of data represents the immediate reaction to the program from a variety of key stakeholders, particularly participants who have the responsibility to make it work. At this level, a variety of basic reaction measures are taken, often representing five to 15 separate measures to gain insight into the value, importance, relevance, and usefulness of the employee engagement programs.

Learning Data

As the employee engagement programs continue, new information is acquired and new skills are learned. This level of measurement (Level 2) focuses on the changes in knowledge and skill acquisition, and details what still needs to be learned. Some programs have a high learning component, such as job design. Others may have a low learning component, such as brief engagement sessions. In some cases, the focus is on organizational learning or departmental skill development.

Application and Implementation Data

Application and implementation are key measures that show the extent to which employees are engaged, behavior has changed, and employee performance has improved. This type of data reflects how actions are taken, adjustments are made, new skills are applied, habits are changed, and steps in a new process are initiated as a result of the employee engagement programs.

This is one of the most powerful categories because it uncovers not only the extent to which the employee engagement programs are implemented, but also the reasons for lack of success. At this level, barriers and enablers to application and implementation are detailed, and a complete profile of performance change at the various steps of implementation is provided.

Business Impact Data (Tangible and Intangible)

As employees become more engaged, behavior change or actions taken in application and implementation have consequences. These can be described in one or more me sures representing an influence on the work environment, such as a direct impact to an individual, team, or department, or as an impact to other parts of the organization.

This level of data (Level 4) reflects the specific business impact and may include measures—such as output, quality, costs, time, job satisfaction, and customer satisfaction—that have been influenced by the application and implementation of the employee engagement program. A direct link between the business impact and the program must be established for the program to drive business value. At this level of analysis, a technique must be used to isolate the effects of the program from other influences that may be driving the same measure. Answering the following question is imperative: How do you know it was the employee engagement program that caused the improvement and not something else?

Chain of Value

Intangible data consist of measures that are not converted to monetary value. In some cases, converting certain measures to monetary values is not credible with a reasonable amount of resources. In these situations, data are listed as an intangible, but only if they are linked to the engagement program.

ROI Data

This level of measurement compares the monetary value of the business impact measures with the actual cost of the program. It is the ultimate level of accountability and represents the financial impact directly linked with the program, expressed as a benefit-cost ratio (BCR) or return-on-investment percentage. This measure is the fifth level of evaluation. It requires converting business impact data to monetary value and comparing that value with the fully loaded cost of the program.

Satisfaction leads to learning, which leads to application, which leads to business impact, and ultimately to return on investment. At the business impact level, the effects of the program must be isolated from other influences. In addition, business impact data are converted to monetary value and compared with the cost of the program to develop the return on investment. Exhibit 2-3 shows this connection as a chain of impact, which is necessary to drive business value. Stakeholders will more readily understand this chain of impact as they consider the long-term success of employee engagement. It is a novel yet pragmatic way to show results.

Fortunately, the ROI Methodology works extremely well in all types of environments and projects. The first level is critical, as a program would likely be unsuccessful if an adverse reaction occurred. An element of learning is also required to make a program successful: Those participating usually acquire knowledge and skills, and some projects even require significant skill development. However, learning does not guarantee success. Follow-up is needed to ensure that the knowledge and skills are being used appropriately. Therefore, application and implementation are critical for effectiveness; failure in these areas is typically what causes program failure overall.

The most important data set for those who sponsor projects is the impact, which is the consequence of application and is often expressed in business terms as output, quality, costs, and time. However, showing the impact of a program isn't enough for some executives. They want the ultimate level of accountability: return on investment. ROI converts the amount of the improvement at the impact level (attributed to the program) to money, and compares that with the cost of the program.

Exhibit 2-3. Chain of Impact

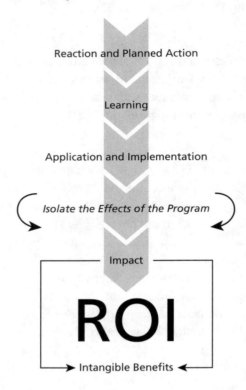

Reaction and Planned Action

Learning

Application and Implementation

Isolate the Effects of the Program

Impact

ROI

Intangible Benefits

SELECTING PROGRAMS FOR ROI ANALYSIS

Every employee engagement program should be evaluated in some way, even if it's only collecting reaction data from those involved in the program. Reaction data alone may be sufficient for evaluating some programs, but the challenge is to collect additional data at higher levels, and to do so only when it is relevant and feasible.

Appropriate evaluation levels are usually determined when the program is initiated, recognizing that the evaluation level may change throughout the life of the program. If the cost of the program increases, sponsors may ask for an evaluation of the impact (Level 4) or even ROI (Level 5) of the program. Because of the resources required and the realistic barriers for ROI implementation, ROI analysis should be used only for those programs that are very expensive, linked to strategic objectives, important for solving organizational problems, and highly visible.

A comprehensive employee engagement program usually meets most, if not all, of these criteria. Deciding which type of evaluation to use is sometimes a trade-off depending on the resources available and the amount of disruption allowed for collecting the data. Because some data collection at this level may disrupt work at varying degrees or inconvenience those involved in some way, the evaluation needs to be balanced with the time, effort, and resources that can be committed to the process. Many organizations fall short of the ideal evaluation, instead settling for a feasible approach within existing constraints.

ROI PROCESS MODEL

Measurement and evaluation must be systematic, following a routine process that can be duplicated in a variety of projects. The ROI Process Model is a 10-step process, illustrated in Exhibit 2-4 (on the next page). The process begins with the end in mind by creating objectives, and proceeds until an impact report is generated. It is highly adaptable to the needs of the project in question and the evaluation can stop at any point along the process. The data collected during the program at Level 1 and Level 2, and data collected after the program at Levels 3 and 4, are steps along the way. This process will be explained in further detail in chapters 3 through 6.

FINAL THOUGHTS

This chapter presented a measurement culture and explained why that culture is so important in the context of employee engagement. Building on the premise that a measurement culture matters, this chapter explored ways for employee engagement practitioners to become change agents and build a measurement culture within the organizations in which they work. Finally, an introduction to the ROI Methodology was provided as a process to build a measurement culture.

Exhibit 2-4. ROI Methodology Process Model

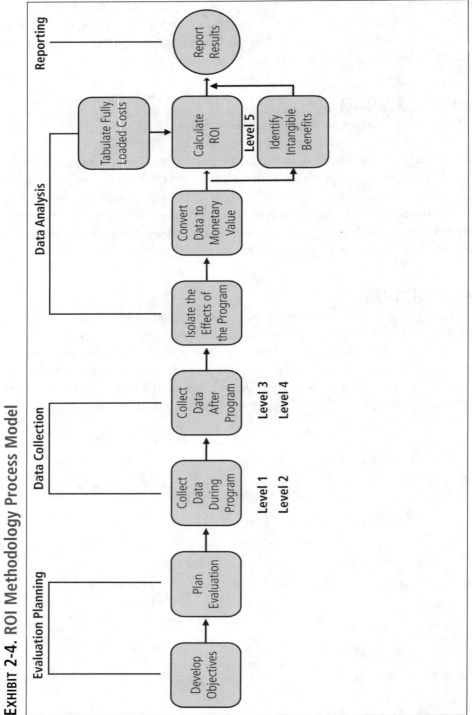

3

Alignment of Engagement Programs and Evaluation Planning

I n far too many situations, employee engagement programs are implemented without a complete picture of the reason for the program. Pursuing initiatives without knowing why or identifying clear performance and business needs up front can be disastrous in today's economic climate. Evaluation is too often an afterthought. This chapter explores why it is important to plan ahead, how to use the V-Model to align programs with business needs, the process of integrating needs with the evaluation, and the steps and artifacts included in evaluation planning.

ACHIEVING THE PROPER ALIGNMENT

The basis for an employee engagement program adding value rests on the rationale for its existence and the extent to which it relates to a specific business need. This fundamental concept requires a thorough needs analysis, which is the beginning point in the ROI Methodology. As described in chapter 2, conducting a diagnosis or assessment of the organization's needs allows the employee engagement practitioner to determine, with the help of the client, the necessary programs. This also sets the stage for collecting any necessary data and minimizing defensiveness and resistance.

There are a variety of methods for conducting a needs analysis, but integrating the ROI Methodology is critical when measuring at higher levels of evaluation. For example, let's assume that during an analysis phase two findings emerge: high turnover and low productivity. This is where the analysis phase moves to inquiring about what behaviors, rewards, and helpful mechanisms may be contributing to the high turnover and decreased productivity. In this case, a lack of employee engagement is causing most of the problems, but the organization's leaders are not aware of how serious the problem is. The solution involves increasing engagement and developing leaders who use and encourage engagement in productive ways. As you can see, this approach not only helps identify the right solution, but it sets into motion relevant goals and measures. There are two key questions that help quantify the gap that exists: What is the ideal or desired state? What is the current state?

The V-Model is a powerful method for ensuring business alignment because it maps the connection of needs analysis from programs to objectives and evaluation

(Exhibit 3-1). It shows the important links between the evaluation and the initial problem or opportunity that created the need for the program. It also shows the three points at which business alignment occurs—the beginning of the program, during the program, and during the follow-up evaluation—in order to validate the alignment.

EXHIBIT 3-1. Alignment With the V-Model

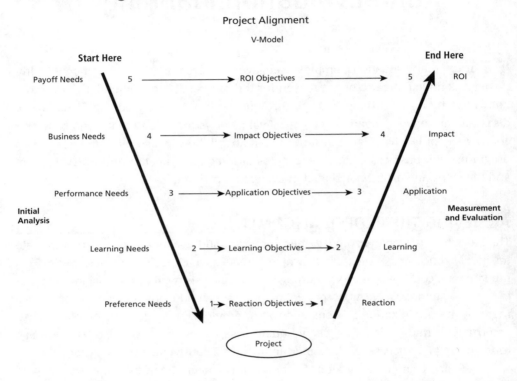

The V-Model is based on the concept of the five levels of evaluation described in chapter 2. As we will explore throughout this book, employee engagement is a natural candidate for the ROI Methodology and its alignment process.

It's best to think of the V-Model in terms of the evaluation side first. Evaluation moves through different levels of measurement:

- reaction to the engagement concept (Level 1)
- learning how to be engaged (Level 2)
- application; becoming engaged (Level 3)
- impact; the consequences of engagement measured through output, quality, and time (Level 4)
- ROI; the financial value of engagement, a comparison of monetary benefits with the cost of the program (Level 5).

From the viewpoint of key stakeholders, such as the clients or sponsors, the higher levels are more important because they show the business contribution (Level 4) and ROI (Level 5). In terms of evaluation, Level 4 is where an isolation technique is applied to specify how much improvement comes directly from the program. This step ensures that business alignment is confirmed.

The measures that are captured at each level are defined in the objectives. There are five corresponding levels of objectives, as illustrated in Exhibit 3-1, which increase in importance as the levels progress; Levels 4 and 5 are often the most valuable from a client's perspective. These objectives are developed during the needs assessment, which defines particular needs at each level. Here, the highest and most important level is the potential payoff of the program, followed by business, performance, learning, and preference needs.

Level 5, Payoff Needs

Needs assessment occurring at Level 5 addresses the potential payoff opportunity for an organization. This step is taken to determine whether an ROI will be possible if the program is pursued. The first part of the process is to decide whether the problem is worth solving or if the opportunity warrants serious consideration. This is obvious in cases where serious problems are affecting the organization's operations and strategy. For example, reversing an annual 32 percent turnover rate of critical talent at a hospital is an obvious payoff opportunity. Another example is an organization for which new account growth is flat and customer loyalty is low based on industry standards. These types of payoff opportunities make it clear that there is a problem that needs to be solved or an opportunity that should be pursued with a clearly identified business need.

Others represent not-so-obvious payoff opportunities, such as a request to implement an employee engagement program or a succession management process. In this case, the business measures of significance become more evident during the Level 4 analysis.

During Level 5 analysis, it is important to not only identify the business measures that need to improve, but also convert them into monetary values when possible so the anticipated economic benefit of addressing the opportunity is evident. Determining the payoff's monetary value is useful not only in identifying the scope of the opportunity, but also in forecasting the potential ROI. In many situations, this may not be a calculation but an "estimate" based on the perception of the cost of having disengaged employees. When the solution(s) is identified and the targets for improvement as a result of the solution are set, it is important to determine the approximate cost for the entire project. With the approximate program cost and the monetary value of the opportunity in hand, you can use the ROI forecast to indicate the potential payoff for investing in a particular program. While this practice may not be feasible for some programs, it is often important and necessary for very expensive, strategic, or critical programs.

Level 4, Business Needs

At Level 4, business data that indicate movement toward addressing the payoff need are examined to determine which measures are in most need of improvement. Ideally, employee engagement should improve the business measures listed in Exhibits 3-2 and 3-3. When cross-functional programs are anticipated, each participant could have a different business need. This may involve having participants bring one, two, or three measures (business needs) to improve, using the competencies with their teams. This is very powerful because employee engagement is now customized to the participants at the impact level.

EXHIBIT 3-2. Examples of Hard Data

Output	Quality	Costs	Time
• Completion rate	• Failure rates	• Shelter costs	• Cycle time
• Units produced	• Dropout rates	• Treatment costs	• Equipment downtime
• Tons manufactured	• Scrap	• Budget variances	
• Items assembled	• Waste	• Unit costs	• Overtime
• Money collected	• Rejects	• Cost by account	• On-time shipments
• Items sold	• Error rates	• Variable costs	• Time to project completion
• New accounts generated	• Rework	• Fixed costs	
• Forms processed	• Shortages	• Overhead costs	• Processing time
• Loans approved	• Product defects	• Operating costs	• Setup time
• Inventory turnover	• Deviation from standard	• Program cost savings	• Time to proficiency
• Patients visited	• Product failures	• Accident costs	• Learning time
• Applications processed	• Inventory adjustments	• Program costs	• Meeting schedules
• Students graduated	• Time card corrections	• Sales expense	• Repair time
• Tasks completed	• Incidents	• Participant costs	• Efficiency
• Output per hour	• Compliance discrepancies		• Work stoppages
• Productivity	• Agency fees		• Order response
• Work backlog			• Late reporting
• Incentive bonus			• Lost time

This process may involve reviewing organizational databases to examine all types of hard and soft data. Sometimes the performance of one item triggers the employee engagement program. For example, it's easy to pinpoint the business measure when sales are not as high as they should be, operating costs are excessive, product quality is deteriorating, or productivity is low. These key measures come directly from data in the organization and are often found in the operating databases.

Exhibit 3-3. Examples of Soft Data

Work Habits	Customer Service	Work Climate/ Satisfaction	Employee Development and Advancement
• Tardiness • Visits to the dispensary • Violations of safety rules • Communication breakdowns • Excessive breaks	• Customer complaints • Customer dissatisfaction • Customer impressions • Customer loyalty • Customer retention • Customer value • Lost customers	• Grievances • Discrimination charges • Employee complaints • Job satisfaction • Organization commitment • Employee engagement • Employee loyalty • Intent to leave • Stress	• Promotions • Capability • Intellectual capital • Programs completed • Requests for transfer • Performance appraisal ratings • Readiness • Networking

Exhibit 3-2 shows these business needs arranged into four hard data categories: output, quality, costs, and time. Examples include sales, production, errors, waste, accidental costs, downtime, project time, and compliance fines. These measures exist in any type of organization—even in the public sector and among nonprofits and non-government organizations—and often attract the attention of executives and chief administrators because they represent business impact. It is important to connect a project to at least one of these measures. However, keep in mind that impact measures can also be subjective, such as customer service, image, work climate, customer satisfaction, job satisfaction, engagement, reputation, and teamwork.

In other cases, business alignment with employee engagement programs may involve a review of HR measures, such as employee engagement, job satisfaction, employee complaints and grievances, absenteeism and tardiness, teamwork, accidents and incidents, performance ratings, employee transfers and promotions, and talent retention, turnover, and turnover costs. Although these measures may not be as important as measures of output, quality, costs, and time, they are still important, and in some cases are the primary measures of interest for an employee engagement program. Soft data are sometimes reported as a program's intangible benefits because they cannot always be converted to money credibly or with a minimum amount of resources. But they can be important business measures and, if improved, can help an organization take advantage of a payoff opportunity.

Level 3, Performance Needs

The Level 3 analysis involves determining performance needs or gaps that will contribute to improving the business measures. The task is to determine what is causing the problem (or creating the opportunity) identified at Level 4; for example, what is causing the business to be performing below the desired level? What should the organization be doing more or less of? Is there something the organization should be doing differently? Performance tools or systems, inadequate technology, lack of engagement, and broken or ineffective processes are all examples of performance needs.

The desired and current state should reveal performance needs because the reason for the inadequate performance will be the basis for the solution. For example, if customer complaints have increased, and it is discovered that the technology used by customer service is outdated and slow, then the technology that supports customer service representatives is the cause of the problem and needs to be resolved.

Performance needs can be uncovered using a variety of problem-solving or analysis techniques. This may involve the use of data collection techniques, such as surveys, questionnaires, focus groups, or interviews. The key is to determine the causes of the problem so that solutions can be developed. Sometimes there is one clear solution to address the performance need; other times there are multiple solutions and then a decision must be made as to which one to pursue, if pursuing all is not an option. ROI forecasting is one way to help make the decision.

Level 2, Learning Needs

During the Level 2 assessment, the specific information, knowledge, or skills required to address the performance needs are identified. An analysis may reveal learning deficiencies, in terms of knowledge and skills that can contribute to the problem. In other situations, the solution will need a learning component as employees learn how to implement a new process, procedure, or technology. For employee engagement, the solution typically involves the acquisition of knowledge or the development of skills necessary to become more engaged. In some cases, perceptions or attitudes may need to be altered before an employee engagement program can be successful. The extent of learning required will determine whether formalized training is needed, or if more informal, on-the-job methods can be used to create an increased engagement.

Level 1, Preference Needs

Finally, the Level 1 assessment describes the preferences for the engagement program. This involves determining the preferred way in which those involved in the process will need or want it to be implemented. Typical questions that surface include "Is this important?" "Is this necessary?" and "Is it relevant to me?" Preference needs may involve aspects of implementation, including decisions about when learning is expected, in what amounts, how it is presented, and the overall timeframe. Implementation involves timing, support, expectations, and other key factors.

Using the V-Model, Exhibit 3-4 shows an example of linking needs assessment with the evaluation of an employee engagement program involving a team-based process for making improvements. The target audience is composed of team members and team leaders. As the exhibit shows, the first step is to see if the problem is worth pursuing.

These five levels of needs analysis develop a comprehensive profile for determining how best to address an opportunity or problem worth solving. They also serve as the basis for the engagement program objectives.

Exhibit 3-4. Employee Engagement Program Example With the V-Model

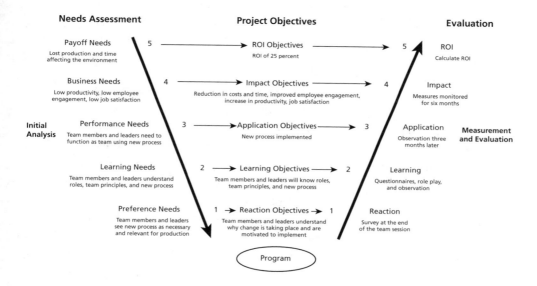

Objectives

Objectives keep the employee engagement program and the business aligned by positioning that program with the outcomes in mind at every level. The levels of objectives are:

- Level 0 Input objectives are the indicators that are generally tracked, such as the number of programs, people affected, hours, and so on. They are categorized as Level 0 because they do not reflect the outcome.
- Level 1 Reaction and planned action objectives describe expected immediate satisfaction with the employee engagement program. They define important

aspects, including the relevance of the change and the importance of the information or content shared through the process.

- Level 2 Learning objectives describe the expected immediate outcomes in terms of knowledge acquisition, skill attainment, awareness, and insights gained through the employee engagement program. These objectives set the stage for transitioning to performance and behavior change.
- Level 3 Application objectives describe the expected intermediate outcomes in terms of what behavior change, involvement, and actions are expected as a result of the employee engagement program. Objectives may target specific steps to be taken or specific behaviors that need to change.
- Level 4 Impact objectives define the specific business measures that should improve as a result of the employee engagement. Improvements in these intermediate (and sometimes long-term) outcomes represent changes in output, quality, costs, and time, as well as customer satisfaction and employee satisfaction. Objectives at this level answer the question, "So what?" as it relates to the program. They describe to stakeholders the importance of the intervention.
- Level 5 ROI objectives define for stakeholders the intended financial outcome. This single indicator sets the expectation for how the benefits of the employee engagement program will relate to the cost. These objectives must be identified and developed before the evaluation can be conducted; ideally this occurs early in the process when the program is being designed.

Each level represents a category of measures that describes how much progress is being made to address the various levels of need. Specific measurable objectives serve as the blueprint for building the employee engagement program. By aligning initiatives with the business through a thorough needs assessment and the development of measurable objectives, the implementation and evaluation of the employee engagement program becomes more systematic and reliable. Identifying stakeholder needs and developing relevant objectives make up the first two phases of business alignment and set the stage for planning the third phase: evaluation.

Case in Point

In this example, the payoff need is based on the problem of lost production time and damage to the work environment. To understand the impact (Level 4), the problem must be examined in more detail: While the average production time is at an all-time high, productivity levels have not increased in the last 18 months. The pressure of not meeting departmental and organization goals is putting stress on employees and has affected job satisfaction and employee engagement. When all these measures are considered it becomes obvious that there is a business problem worth solving.

With the confirmation at Level 4 that there are business needs, a potential payoff can be projected. This involves estimating the cost of lost productivity and time, and using standard values for production and time to determine the improvements that can come from the project. This develops a profile of potential payoff and further demonstrates why the problem is worth solving.

At Level 3, the causes of the problem are explored using a variety of techniques, and each measure needs to be analyzed to see what factors are causing its current status. (For example, why is productivity not improving, or what is the cause of the job dissatisfaction?) For this project, the analysts conducted interviews and focus groups to understand why business measures were at their current level. The key principle, as in any analysis, is to identify the potential solution to the problem. A new team engagement process was seen as a viable option for organizing the work in teams. The potential impact was to dramatically reduce the time it took to produce new products. The program also needed to include soft skills because the employee base was not accustomed to working in teams—team leaders and members would learn new behaviors that were associated with team engagement and performance.

At Level 2, learning is explored. Do team leaders and members understand the new process? Are they clear about their new roles? The new process and team roles were at the heart of the learning needs.

At Level 1, the desired reaction is considered. A realistic picture of the change involved must be shared so that teams understand the relevance of the approach. Adapting to change, motivation to implement, and the importance of the new process are factors that are critical to the success of launching this approach.

EVALUATION PLANNING

The evaluation must be planned—overall and individually—for each program. Not much planning is involved for an evaluation conducted only at the reaction levels, but as the evaluation moves up the value chain, increased attention and effort needs to be placed on planning. During the typical planning cycle, the purpose of the evaluation must be reviewed for specific solutions and to determine where the evaluation will stop on the value chain. The feasibility of evaluating at different levels should also be explored.

Employee engagement professionals understand the importance of planning for almost any type of undertaking. Most agree that thorough planning can lead to more effective implementation. The same holds true for ROI analysis. Careful planning for ROI analysis not only saves time and effort, but can also make a difference in the success or failure of the entire project. Planning involves the development of three documents: data collection plan, ROI analysis plan, and communication and implementation plan. These documents are described using the following case study.

CASE STUDY

A manufacturing company with 15,000 employees has experienced some recent problems. Revenues have increased during the past three years, but profit margins have declined to breakeven. The company has a solid and loyal customer base and aligns the business to client needs. However, the executive team is concerned about high turnover rates, low productivity, and low employee engagement. A recent analysis of the annual engagement survey determined several key outcomes:

- To grow the business, more leaders need to ensure that employees are engaged.
- Employees need to have a clear understanding of their goals.
- Employees are not sure of their responsibilities.

The lack of engagement was also linked to business needs, including productivity, quality, retention, and cost reduction. The employee engagement team determined that it would be beneficial to the company to use team leaders to drive employee engagement, especially since the competencies identified for leadership included communication skills, business acumen, and the ability to engage employees.

The solution was a three-day intensive learning workshop for team leaders that focused on the concepts of engagement and how team leaders could get their employees more engaged. The employee engagement team agreed to implement a feedback process with the team leaders, which would provide an engagement score before the program and three months after the program to show the changes with this immediate group. The evaluation acted as a control group to isolate the program's effects.

The workshop involved several key steps. Before participating, team leaders completed a one-hour online session to learn about the engagement process. Feedback was administered online and collected from team members and team leaders. This was followed by a feedback session conducted during the three-day workshop, along with a comprehensive report for each leader. The expected outcome was an action plan generated by the team leader.

Objectives

The employee engagement team created the following multilevel objectives for the employee engagement program:

- Participants will rate the employee engagement program as relevant to their jobs.

- Participants will rate the employee engagement as important to their success.
- Participants must demonstrate acceptable performance on setting goals.
- Participants must demonstrate acceptable performance on communicating responsibilities to team members.
- Participants will use the engagement concepts with team members on a routine basis.
- Participants will improve productivity, quality, retention, and costs.

Data Collection Plan

Exhibit 3-5 shows the completed data collection plan. Defining the objectives and measures at each level, including return on investment, is vital. Measures can sometimes be examined in different ways, so defining them up front eliminates confusion.

The data collection methods detailed in Exhibit 3-5 correspond to the different objective levels, using a range of options that are described in the next chapter. Next, the data sources were identified. Data can be collected from existing organizational databases, or by those participating in the employee engagement program. In some cases—as in the case of the 360-degree feedback assessment—team leaders, as well as their direct reports (team members), provide data.

Timing is important for determining when data should be collected from the different sources for each level. During implementation, data often come directly from those involved in the program. In other situations, the follow-up can be determined based on when the program is operational and successful.

Finally, the responsibilities were detailed, outlining specifically who should be involved in the data collection process.

ROI Analysis Plan

Exhibit 3-6 shows the completed ROI analysis plan, which is connected through business impact data. The first column shows the detailed definition of each impact data measure. The second column defines the method for isolating the effects of the program on each data item using one or more of the specific techniques available. The method of converting data to monetary values is listed in the third column using one or more available techniques.

The fourth column defines the cost categories for the specific program. Using a fully loaded cost profile, all the categories are detailed here. Completing this action during the planning stage is helpful for determining whether specific cost categories need to be monitored during implementation. The fifth column defines the intangible benefits that may be derived from the program. When listed here, the intangible benefits are only anticipated; they must be measured in some way to determine whether they have actually been influenced by the program. Finally, the last columns detail other influences that may affect implementation and offer a space for additional comments, respectively.

EXHIBIT 3-5. Data Collection Plan

Intervention: <u>Employee Engagement Program</u>   Responsibility: _____   Date: _____

Level	Objective(s)	Measures/Data	Data Collection Method	Data Sources	Timing	Responsibilities
1	**REACTION/PLANNED ACTION** • Relevance to job • Importance to their success • Action items to improve engagement	• Average of 4 on 5-point scale	• Questionnaire	• Team leaders	• Immediately following the program and the first feedback	• Engagement team
2	**LEARNING** • Engagement concepts • Set goals with team members • Communicate responsibilities • Enhancing leadership skills • Improving engagement	• Average of 4 on 5-point scale	• Questionnaire	• High-potential leaders	• Immediately following the program	• Facilitator
3	**APPLICATION** • Use leadership competencies • Utilize engagement concepts with team members routinely as evidenced by scores on second administration of feedback	• Checklist for action plan • 4 out of 5 on a 5-point scale	• Action plan • Feedback scores	• High-potential leaders • Supervisors, direct reports, peers	• Three months after the program administer it a second time	• Facilitator • HR

4	**BUSINESS IMPACT** • Productivity • Quality • Retention • Cost reduction	• Reduce specific variable costs • Decrease in voluntary turnover • Increase gross productivity • Increase quality (specific measures)	• HR database • Operational database	• Team leaders	• Six months after the program	• HR team
5	**ROI** • 25%					

Comments: Action plans are provided and explained. Team leaders commit to completing action plans and sharing copy with engagement team.

EXHIBIT 3-6. ROI Analysis Plan

Program: Employee Engagement Program   **Responsibility:** _____   **Date:** _____

Data Items (Usually Level 4)	Methods for Isolating the Effects of the Program	Methods of Converting Data to Monetary Values	Cost Categories	Intangible Benefits	Communication Targets for Final Report	Other Influences and Issues During Application	Comments
• Cost reduction • Productivity • Quality • Retention	• Control group • Participant estimates (for backup)	• Standard values	• Diagnostics • Development • Feedback fees • Time of those involved in process • Administrative overhead • Communication expenses • Facilities • Evaluation	• Increased job satisfaction • Increased engagement • Increased teamwork	• Executives • Sponsors • HR team • Team leaders • Team members	• An initiative that may influence the impact measures of the employee engagement program	

Communication and Implementation Plan

The communication and implementation plan details how the results will be communicated to various groups, which groups will receive the information, and the specific schedule of events and activities connected to the other planning documents. It should include the method of communicating, the content of the communication, and the timing for the communication. The plan also defines the rationale for communicating with the group and for anticipated payoffs, along with the individual responsibility for monitoring actions from the evaluation. It clearly delivers the information to the right groups to ensure that action occurs; in almost every impact study there are significant actions that can be taken.

FINAL THOUGHTS

This chapter explored the alignment of employee engagement and evaluation planning. It described in detail when and how an ROI analysis should be considered as a process improvement tool. Using the V-Model, a step-by-step explanation was provided to properly align employee engagement programs with business needs. Special attention was paid to integrating needs analysis with the ROI Methodology, ensuring that the employee engagement practitioner has adequate tools and understanding to conduct a needs assessment and plan for the evaluation. Finally, the role of planning for an ROI project was presented, detailing the key steps in the process through an actual case study and illustrating how planning documents are used.

4

Data Collection at All Levels

For many employee engagement practitioners with psychometrics and industrial psychology in their background, data collection is based on behavioral science methods. Data collection has relevance throughout the program cycle, beginning with diagnostics and ending with follow-up. The primary objective of data collection is to systematically gather information at three significant times: before, to understand organization problems and record hypotheses; during, to collect reaction and learning data; and after, to confirm the effectiveness of the program by collecting application and impact data. This chapter explores data collection methods, principles, and timing. Particular attention is given to collecting data for ROI analysis, and introducing questions to gather estimates for ROI calculation.

QUANTITATIVE AND QUALITATIVE DATA

There are advantages and disadvantages to both quantitative and qualitative methods of research. However, before presenting the methods, it is helpful to discuss the different types of data and research issues.

Advantages to Quantitative Data

Quantitative results have the advantage of being able to provide numerical values for large amounts of data, as well as permitting the use of more powerful methods of mathematical and statistical analysis. Some professionals argue that quantitative data are the only data—they posit that everything is either a zero or one. Quantitative data can help form conclusions by assigning value from attributes to numerical scales and defined categories, and is more easily analyzed with software systems such as Excel or SPSS.

Advantages to Qualitative Data

Qualitative data also have advantages, such as allowing clients to use their own words to describe organization factors and problems. This method is helpful in situations in which the practitioner has a general sense of what to look for, but does not know any details or specifics about an organization. That is why employee engagement practitioners find qualitative interviews and focus groups particularly helpful when beginning a project. Qualitative data provide a richness, depth, and complexity that may be unique to the measurement culture. It is important to consider culture and its implication for data collection.

Organization Culture Implications

An organization's culture may have implications for data collection methods. For some organizations, surveys are considered impersonal and bothersome, such as when employees are constantly being surveyed with no clear thought around the timing or methods for collecting data. Other organizations may be feedback deprived. This observation alone may be worth exploring, because there may be underlying assumptions about the means of communication within the organization.

Another consideration is whether to provide confidential or anonymous surveys. Online surveys allow for anonymity in providing input, which could be a critical point to consider in the context of organization culture. Some groups have found that by offering anonymous questionnaires, it not only helps to improve response rates, but provides richer and more comprehensive data.

Mixing It Up

Mixed methodology allows for a combined qualitative and quantitative approach. This tactic is often used in creating questionnaires. In this case, the qualitative method precedes the quantitative by gathering important details that will help form the questions and response options for the questionnaire. For example, an employee engagement practitioner in one company conducted employee interviews to collect specific perceptions and feedback. When the interview data were organized and analyzed, the employee engagement practitioner created a questionnaire based on the findings. In this way, the hypotheses could be confirmed and helped target the questionnaire to gather generalizable findings.

Resource Implications

Many companies rely on quantitative methods because data collection and analysis processes can be automated through online-hosted survey systems. This may mean more up-front work to create meaningful questions, but in cases with simple analysis and reporting, automating this process can drastically reduce the required effort. Questionnaires also allow the practitioner to collect sample data that are representative of the populations, and using proper analytical tools, infer generalizations about the larger population or organization as a whole.

QUESTIONNAIRES AND SURVEYS

The most common method of data collection is the questionnaire. Ranging from short reaction forms to detailed follow-up tools, questionnaires are used to obtain subjective information about the organization or group involved, as well as objective data to measure business results for ROI analysis. With its versatility and popularity, the questionnaire is an optimal method for capturing the first four levels of data (reaction, learning, application, and business impact). Surveys represent a specific type of questionnaire to capture attitudes, beliefs, and opinions. The principles of survey construction and design are similar to questionnaire design. A questionnaire may include any of the following types of items:

- An open-ended question has an unlimited answer. The question is followed by ample blank space for the response.
- A checklist provides a list of items in which respondents are asked to check those that apply in the situation.
- A two-way question has alternate responses (yes or no) or other possibilities.
- A multiple-choice question asks the respondent to select the most applicable response.
- A ranking scale requires the respondent to rank a list of items.

Questionnaire design is a straightforward, logical process. The following steps help develop a valid, reliable, and effective instrument:

1. Determine the specific information needed for each domain or level.
2. Secure input from subject matter experts.
3. Involve management in the process when appropriate and feasible.
4. Decide on the method for returning the questionnaire.
5. Select the type(s) of questions. Keep in mind the time needed for analysis.
6. Choose the first question carefully.
7. Group related questions.
8. Begin with easy questions and build to more complex ones.
9. Present the questions in the order of the results chain of impact.
10. Place sensitive questions at the end of the questionnaire.
11. Develop the questions with clarity and simplicity in mind.
12. Draft the questionnaire, checking the flow and total length.
13. Check the reading level and match it to the audience.
14. Design for ease of tabulation and analysis.
15. Be consistent in the visual presentation of the questions.
16. Use color and contrast to help respondents recognize the components of the questionnaire without distracting from the items themselves.
17. Avoid clutter and complexity in the question.
18. Develop the revised questionnaire.
19. Test the questions with a small group of individuals who are knowledgeable about the target audience.
20. Keep responses anonymous or confidential.
21. Finalize the completed questionnaire and prepare a data summary.
22. Use an existing user-friendly software tool if feasible.

The areas of feedback used on reaction questionnaires depend on the purpose of the evaluation. Some forms are simple, while others are detailed and require considerable time to complete. When a comprehensive evaluation is planned, and impact and ROI are being measured, the reaction questionnaire can be simple, asking only questions that provide pertinent information about an individual's perception of the program. However, when a reaction questionnaire is the only means of collecting evaluation data, a more comprehensive list of questions is necessary. This feedback can be useful in making adjustments to an organization, assisting in predicting performance after the program, or both.

In most medium to large organizations with significant employee engagement, reaction instruments are automated for analysis and reporting. Some organizations use direct input into a website to develop detailed reports and databases, which allows feedback data to be compared with other programs.

Collecting learning data with a questionnaire is also common. Simple questions to measure learning can be developed for inclusion in the reaction questionnaire or in the form of a test. There are several possible areas to explore on a questionnaire aimed at measuring learning, including change in perception or attitude, knowledge gain, skill enhancement, ability, capability, and awareness. Questions to gauge learning are developed using a format similar to the reaction part of the questionnaire. They measure the extent to which learning has taken place.

Questionnaires are also commonly used to collect post-program application and impact data. Reaction and learning data may also be captured in a follow-up questionnaire to compare with similar data gathered immediately following the intervention. Most follow-up issues, however, involve application and implementation (Level 3) and business impact (Level 4):

- use of materials, guides, and technology
- application of knowledge and skills
- frequency of use of knowledge and skills
- success with use of knowledge and skills
- change in work or work behavior
- improvements and accomplishments
- monetary impact of improvements
- improvements linked to the intervention
- confidence level of data supplied
- perceived value of the investment
- linkage with output measures
- barriers to implementation
- enablers to implementation
- management support for implementation

- other benefits
- other possible solutions
- target audience recommendations.

TESTING

Testing can be important for measuring learning in employee engagement evaluations. Preprogram and post-program tests are an effective way to measure the change in learning. An improvement in test scores shows the change in skill, knowledge, or attitude attributed to the program. Performance testing, simulations, role plays, and business games are used to measure the extent of the skills gained related to a program.

INTERVIEWS

Another helpful data collection method is the interview. The employee engagement team or a third party usually conducts the interview, which can secure data not available in business or organization databases or data that may be difficult to obtain through written responses or observations. Interviews can also uncover success stories that can be useful in communicating evaluation results. Participants may be reluctant to describe their results in a questionnaire, but may be willing to volunteer the information to a skillful interviewer who uses probing techniques. The interview process can uncover reaction, learning, and impact data, but it is primarily used during diagnostics and post-program phases. It is particularly useful when gathering application or performance data. However, one major disadvantage of the interview is that it is time-consuming because it requires interviewer preparation to ensure the process is consistent, as well as thematic analysis afterward.

Interviews are categorized into two basic types: structured and unstructured. A structured interview is much like a questionnaire. The interviewer asks specific questions that allow the interviewee little room to deviate from the menu of expected responses. The structured interview offers several advantages over the questionnaire. For example, an interview can ensure that the questions are answered and that the interviewer understands the responses supplied by the interviewee. The unstructured interview has built-in flexibility to allow the interviewer to probe for additional information. This type of interview uses a small number of core questions that can lead to more detailed information as important data are uncovered. The interviewer must be skilled in interviewing a variety of individuals and using the probing process. Interview design and steps for interviews are similar to those of the questionnaire. Preparing the interviewer, piloting the interview, providing clear instruction to the interviewee, and asking a set of core questions are critical steps in gathering useful data.

FOCUS GROUPS

Similar to interviews, focus groups are helpful when in-depth feedback is needed. A focus group involves a small group discussion conducted by an experienced facilitator, who solicits qualitative feedback on a planned topic. Group members are all invited to provide their thoughts, because individual input builds on group input.

Focus groups have several advantages over questionnaires, surveys, tests, or interviews. The basic premise of using focus groups is that when quality perspectives are subjective, several individual perspectives are better than one. The group process, whereby group members stimulate ideas in others, is an effective method for generating qualitative data. Focus groups are less expensive than individual interviews and can be quickly planned and conducted. They should be small (eight to 12 individuals) and should consist of a representative sample of the target population. Group facilitators should have expertise in conducting focus groups with a wide range of individuals. The flexibility of this data collection method makes it possible to explore organizational matters before the intervention, as well as to collect unexpected outcomes or application after the program. Barriers to implementation can also be explored through focus groups, while collecting examples and real concerns from those involved in the intervention.

Focus groups are particularly helpful when qualitative information about the success of a program is needed. For example, focus groups can be used to:

- Collect information contributing to diagnosis and the proposed solution.
- Gauge the overall effectiveness of program application.
- Identify the barriers and enablers to a successful implementation.
- Isolate the impact of an organization from other influences.

Focus groups are helpful when evaluation information is needed but cannot be collected adequately with questionnaires, interviews, or quantitative methods. It's an inexpensive and quick way to determine the strengths and weaknesses of HR initiatives. However, for a complete evaluation, focus group information should be combined with data from other instruments.

OBSERVATIONS

Another potentially useful data collection method is observation. The observer may be a member of the employee engagement team, an immediate manager, a member of a peer group, or an external party. The most common observer, and probably the most practical, is a member of the employee engagement team.

To be effective, observations need to be systematic and well developed, minimizing the observer's influence and subjectivity. Observers should be carefully selected, fully prepared, and knowledgeable about how to interpret, score (if relevant), and report what they see.

This method is useful for collecting data on employee engagement, leadership development, management training, coaching, and executive education. For example, observation is used to provide 360-degree feedback as behavior changes are solicited from direct reports, colleagues, internal customers, and immediate managers, and through self-input. This is considered a delayed report method of observation. This feedback process can be the actual program, or it could be used before participating in another development initiative.

There are cases when observation is either invisible or unnoticeable. Invisible means that the person under observation is not aware that the observation is taking place, as in the case of a secret shopper. For example, Starbucks uses secret shoppers to observe their employees. A secret shopper goes to one of the stores, takes note of how long orders take to process, the demeanor of the server, whether the store and bathrooms are clean, and whether the server is familiar with new drink offerings. The observation continues immediately following the visit when the secret shopper checks the temperature of his drink order. This observation activity is supposed to be done in a way unbeknownst to the server.

Unnoticeable observations are situations in which the person under observation may know that the observation is taking place, but doesn't notice it because it occurs over a longer period of time or at random times. Examples of unnoticeable observations include listening in on customer service calls ("this call may be monitored for quality assurance purposes") or a 360-degree feedback process.

ACTION PLANS AND PERFORMANCE AGREEMENTS

For many employee engagement programs, business data are readily available. However, data won't always be easily accessible to the program evaluator. Sometimes, data are maintained at an individual, work unit, or department level and may not be known to anyone outside that area. Tracking down those data sets may be too expensive and time-consuming. In these cases, the use of action plans and performance agreements may be helpful for capturing data sets.

Action plans capture application and implementation data; however, this method can also be a useful way to collect business impact data. For business impact data, the action plan is more focused and often deemed more credible than a questionnaire. The performance agreement is an action plan with a preprogram commitment, which means an action plan can easily be converted to a performance agreement with minor adjustments. The main difference between an action plan and a performance agreement is that performance agreements put the dialogue and agreement between a group member and her immediate manager. This can be a powerful process that drives tremendous results, and is appropriate for employee engagement programs where there is a need to achieve improvement. Not only do group members have the content to drive improvement, but they also have the support of their immediate managers and the extra efforts and attention of the facilitator to meet the performance target.

The basic design principles involved in developing and administering action plans are the same for collecting both application and business impact data. The following steps are recommended when an action plan is developed and implemented to capture business impact data and to convert the data to monetary values. The adjustments needed to convert action plans to performance agreements are described at the end of the section.

Set Goals and Targets

As shown in Exhibit 4-1, an action plan can be developed with a direct focus on business impact data. The plan presented in this exhibit requires an overall objective for the plan to be developed, which is usually the primary objective of the employee engagement program. In some cases, an organization may have more than one objective, which requires additional action plans. In addition to the objective, the improvement measure is defined, along with the current and target levels of performance. This information requires the individual to anticipate the application of skills and set goals for specific performances that can be realized.

The action plan is completed during the program, often with input and assistance from an employee engagement team. The practitioner approves the plan, indicating that the action steps meet the requirements of being SMART: specific, motivating, achievable, realistic, and timely. Each plan can be developed in a 30-minute timeframe and often begins with action steps related to the intervention. These action steps are Level 3 activities that detail the application and implementation of employee engagement program content. These steps build support for and are linked to business impact measures.

Defining the Unit of Measure

The next step is to define the actual unit of measure. In some cases more than one measure may be used and will subsequently be contained in additional action plans. The unit of measure is necessary to break the process into the simplest steps so that its ultimate value can be determined. The unit may be output data, such as one unit produced or one closed sale. In terms of quality, the unit can be one reject, one error, or one rework. Time-based units are usually measured in minutes, hours, days, or weeks, such as one hour of process time. Other units are specific to their particular type of data, such as one grievance, one complaint, one absence, or one turnover. Here, simplicity rules the day by breaking down impact data into the simplest terms possible.

EXHIBIT 4-1. Sample Action Plan

Name: _____ Facilitator Signature: _____ Follow-Up Date: _____ Objective: _____

Evaluation Period: _____ to _____ Improvement Measure: _____

Current Performance: _____ Target Performance: _____

Action Steps	Analysis
1. _____ _____	A. What is the unit of measure? _____
2. _____ _____	B. What is the value (cost) of one unit? $ _____
3. _____ _____	C. How did you arrive at this value? _____
4. _____ _____	D. How much did the measure change during the evaluation period? (monthly value) _____
5. _____ _____	E. List the other factors that have influenced this change. _____ _____ _____
6. _____ _____	F. What percentage of this change was actually caused by this program? _____ %
7. _____ _____	G. What level of confidence do you place on the above information? (100%=Certainty and 0%=No Confidence) _____ %
Intangible Benefits:	

Comments: _____

Place a Monetary Value on Each Improvement

During the employee engagement program, those involved are asked to locate, calculate, or estimate the monetary value for each improvement outlined in the plan. The unit value is determined using a variety of methods, such as standard values, expert input, external databases, or estimates.

The process used to arrive at the value is described in the instructions for the action plan. When the actual improvement occurs, these values will be used to capture the annual monetary benefits of the plan. The employee engagement practitioner must be prepared to discuss values and reasonable methods in the session. The preferred method of determining value is to use standard values or expert opinion. However, in the worst-case scenario, those participating in the employee engagement program are asked to estimate the value. When estimates are necessary, it is important to collect the basis of their calculations, so space for this information should be provided.

Implement the Action Plan

Ideally, the action plan is implemented after the program. Action plan steps are followed (Level 3), and subsequent business impact improvements are ensured (Level 4). The results are then forwarded to the engagement team.

Provide Specific Improvements

At the end of the specified follow-up period—usually three months, six months, nine months, or one year—group members indicate the specific improvements they've made. This determines the actual amount of change that has been observed, measured, and recorded. The values are typically expressed as a daily, weekly, or monthly amount, and group members must understand how important accuracy is. In most cases, only the changes are recorded, because those amounts are needed to calculate the monetary values linked to the employee engagement program. In other cases, before and after data may be recorded, which allows the evaluator to calculate the differences.

Isolate the Effects of the Program

Although the action plan is initiated because of the employee engagement program, the actual improvements reported on the action plan may have been influenced by other factors. The program usually shares the credit for the improvement gained. For example, an action plan to implement engagement skills for department managers could only be given partial credit for a business improvement because other variables in the work unit may have influenced the impact measures.

There are several ways to isolate the effects of an employee engagement program, but group member estimation is often used in the action planning process. In this method, group members are asked to estimate the percentage of the improvement that is directly related to the employee engagement program. This question can be asked on the action plan form or in a follow-up questionnaire; sometimes it's beneficial to precede this question with a request to identify all the other factors that may have influenced the results. This allows group members to think through the relationships before allocating a portion to the employee engagement program. Additional detail on methods to isolate the effects of employee engagement programs is presented in chapter 5.

Provide a Confidence Level for Estimates

Isolating the amount of improvement that is directly related to the intervention is not a precise process—it is an estimate. As a result, an error adjustment is made. Group members are asked to indicate their levels of confidence in their estimates using a scale of 0 to 100 percent—0 percent means no confidence and 100 percent means the estimates represent absolute certainty. The confidence estimate serves as an error discount factor.

Collect Action Plans

An excellent response rate is essential, so several steps may be necessary to ensure that the action plans are completed and returned. Group members usually see the importance of the process and develop their plans during the program. Some organizations use follow-up reminders by mail or email. Others call group members to check on their progress. Still others offer assistance in developing the final plan. These steps may require additional resources, which need to be weighed against the importance of having more precise data. Specific ways to improve response rates are discussed later in this chapter.

Summarize the Data and Calculate the ROI

If developed properly, each action plan will have annualized monetary values that are associated with improvements. In addition, each individual will indicate the percentage of the improvement that is directly related to the employee engagement program. Finally, group members provide a confidence estimate expressed as a percentage to reflect their uncertainty with the estimates and the subjective nature of the data they provided.

This process may not appear to be accurate because it involves estimates; however, several adjustments during the analysis make it credible and more accurate. These adjustments reflect the guiding principles of the ROI Methodology, and are outlined in the following.

1. For those group members who do not provide data, the assumption is that they had no improvement to report. This is a very conservative approach.
2. Each value is checked for realism, usability, and feasibility. Extreme values are discarded and omitted from the analysis.

3. Because improvement is annualized, the assumption is that the employee engagement program had no improvement after the first year (for short-term programs). Some add value in the second and third years.

4. The new values are adjusted by the percentage of the improvement that is directly related to the program using multiplication. This isolates the effects of the program.

5. The improvement from step 4 is then adjusted using the confidence estimate, multiplying it by the confidence percentage. The confidence estimate is actually an error percentage suggested by the group participants that is multiplied by the amount of improvement connected to the employee engagement program. For example:

   — A group participant indicates 80 percent confidence reflecting a 20 percent error possibility (100 – 80 = 20).
   — In a $10,000 estimate with an 80 percent confidence factor, the group participant suggests that the value could be in the range of $8,000 to $12,000 (20 percent less to 20 percent more).
   — To be conservative, the lower number, $8,000, is used.

6. The monetary values determined in the previous five steps are totaled to arrive at the final program benefit. Since these values are already annualized, the total of these benefits becomes the annual benefits for the program. This value is placed in the numerator of the ROI formula to calculate the return on investment.

MONITORING PERFORMANCE

One of the more important methods of data collection is monitoring the organization's records. Performance data are available in every organization to report on impact measures such as output, quality, cost, time, job engagement, and customer satisfaction. Most organizations will be able to provide performance data to measure the improvements from an employee engagement program. If not, additional record-keeping systems must be developed for measurement and analysis. At this point, the question of economics arises. Is developing a record-keeping system necessary to evaluate the program economically? If the cost of developing and collecting the data is greater than the expected value for the data, then developing a system to capture the data is meaningless.

The recommended approach is to use existing performance measures, if available. Performance measures should be reviewed to identify the items related to the proposed program objectives. Sometimes, an organization has several performance measures related to the same objective. For example, a new employee engagement program may be designed to increase productivity from the team, which could be measured in a variety of ways:

- team output (products, services, projects)
- individual output
- output per unit of time
- gross productivity (revenue per person)
- time savings (when the saved time is used on other productive work)
- fewer hours worked (with the same output)
- fewer team members (with the same output).

Each of these measures gauges the efficiency or effectiveness of the team. All related measures should be reviewed to determine those most relevant to the employee engagement program.

IMPROVING THE RESPONSE RATE FOR DATA COLLECTION

One of the greatest challenges in data collection is achieving an acceptable response rate. Requiring too much information may result in a suboptimal response rate. The challenge, therefore, is to tackle data collection design and administration so as to achieve the maximum response rate. This is critical when the primary data collection method hinges on input obtained through questionnaires, surveys, and action plans. Here are a few ways to boost response rates:

- Provide advance communication about the questionnaire.
- Clearly communicate the reason for the questionnaire.
- Indicate who will see the results of the questionnaire.
- Show how the data will be integrated with other data.
- Keep the questionnaire as simple as possible.
- Keep questionnaire responses anonymous—or at least confidential.
- Make it easy to respond with email.
- Use two follow-up reminders.
- Have the introduction letter signed by a top executive.
- Send a summary of results to the target audience.
- Have a third party collect and analyze data.
- Communicate the time limit for submitting responses.
- Design questionnaire to attract attention, with a professional format.
- Let group members know what actions will be taken with the data.
- Provide options to respond (such as electronically or paper based).
- Frame questions so group members can respond appropriately to relevant questions.

SOURCES OF DATA

There is an array of possible data sources that can provide input on the success of an employee engagement program. Six general categories are described here.

Business and Operational Databases

Perhaps the most useful and credible data sources for impact and ROI analysis are the databases and reports of the organization. Whether individualized or group based, these records reflect performance in a work unit, department, division, region, or overall organization. Organization databases include all types of measures and are a preferred way to collect data for impact and ROI evaluation because they usually reflect business impact data and are relatively easy to obtain. However, the old adage, "garbage in, garbage out," rings true here. Inconsistent and inaccurate data entry and data processing steps may complicate the task.

Participants

Perhaps the most widely used data source for an ROI analysis is from those participating in the employee engagement program. Participants are a rich source of data for evaluation at the first four levels of data. They are frequently asked about reaction (Level 1), learning (Level 2), and how skills, knowledge, and procedures have been applied on the job (Level 3). Sometimes they are asked to explain the impact or consequence of those actions (Level 4).

Participants are credible because they are involved in the program and are expected to make it successful. They also know the most about other factors that may influence results. The challenge is to find an effective, efficient, and consistent way to capture data from this important source to minimize the time required to provide input.

Participants' Immediate Managers

Another important data source is the participants' immediate supervisor. Managers often have a vested interest in the evaluation process because they approve, support, or require the group members to become involved in the employee engagement program. In many situations, they observe the participants as they attempt to make the intervention successful by applying their new learning.

As a result, managers are able to report on the successes linked to the program, as well as the difficulties and problems associated with application. Although manager input is usually best for application evaluation (Level 3), it can be helpful for impact (Level 4) evaluation. The challenge is to make data collection convenient, efficient, and not disruptive.

Direct Reports

Because most employee engagement programs involve supervisors, managers, and executives, their direct reports can be important sources of data because they can report perceived changes since the program was implemented. Input from direct reports is usually appropriate for application (Level 3) data. For example, in a 360-degree feedback program, comments from direct reports are perhaps the most credible source of data for changes in engagement behavior.

Team or Peer Group

Individuals who serve as team members or occupy peer-level positions in the organization can act as a source of data for some programs. Team or peer group members are usually a source of input for 360-degree feedback. In these situations, peer participants provide input on perceived changes since the program has been implemented. This source is appropriate when all team members participate in the program and, consequently, when they can report on the collective efforts of the group.

Internal or External Groups

In some situations, internal or external groups such as the employee engagement team, program facilitators, coaches, mentors, expert observers, or external consultants may provide input on the success of the individuals when they learn and apply the skills and knowledge covered in the program. Expert observers or assessors may also be used to measure learning. This source may be useful for on-the-job application (Level 3).

TIMING FOR DATA COLLECTION

Another important factor is the timing of data collection. In some cases, prechange measurements are taken to compare with post-change measures, or multiple measures are taken. In other situations, prechange measures are not available and specific follow-ups are still taken after the program. The important issue is to determine the timing for the follow-up evaluation.

The timing of data collection can vary. When a follow-up evaluation is planned after the program, determining the best time for data collection is critical. The challenge is to analyze the nature and scope of the application and implementation, and determine the earliest time that a trend or pattern will evolve. This occurs when the application of skills becomes routine and the implementation is progressing properly. Deciding when to collect data often involves knowing the audience and general time it takes to see change. However, it is important to collect data as early as possible so that potential adjustments can still be made. Evaluations must also allow for behavior changes to occur, so that the application of skills can be observed and measured. Two factors usually determine the routine use of skills: the complexity of the skill and the opportunity to use it. In employee engagement programs spanning a considerable length of time for implementation, measures may be taken at three- to six-month intervals. Using effective measures at well-timed intervals provides successive input on progress and helps to clearly show the extent of improvement.

The timing for impact data collection is based on the delay between application and consequence (the impact). Subject matter experts familiar with this situation should examine the content of the application and implementation and, then considering the context of the work environment, estimate how long it will take for the application to have an impact. In some situations, such as the use of new tools or procedures, the impact may immediately follow the application; in other processes, such as the use of complex leadership skills, the impact may be delayed for some time. For example, managers involved in a program to improve employee engagement will have to learn to work more closely with the team, demonstrating increased caring for the group, assisting team members in achieving individual and professional goals, providing challenging assignments, and allowing team members to learn, grow, and develop. A mere change of behavior will not necessarily result in an immediate reduction in critical talent turnover. There will be some lag between the new behavior and the corresponding increase in retention; however, for most employee engagement programs, the impact usually occurs in a one- to six-month timeframe. The key is to collect the impact data as soon as it occurs.

Convenience and constraints also influence the timing of data collection. If the group members are meeting in a follow-up session or at a special event, that would be an excellent opportunity to collect data. Constraints may be placed on data collection. For example, if sponsors or other executives want the data quickly so they can make decisions about the program, they may move data collection to an earlier-than-ideal time. If this happens, a later data collection will be necessary.

SELECTING THE APPROPRIATE DATA COLLECTION METHOD FOR EACH LEVEL

This chapter presents several data collection methods. Collectively, they offer a wide range of opportunities for collecting data in a variety of situations. Eight specific issues should be considered when deciding which method is appropriate for a situation.

Type of Data

Perhaps one of the most important issues to consider when selecting the method is the type of data to be collected. Some methods are more appropriate for business impact. Follow-up surveys, observations, interviews, focus groups, action planning, and performance contracting are best suited for application data, sometimes exclusively. Performance monitoring, action planning, and questionnaires can easily capture business impact data.

Participant Time for Data Input

Another important factor when selecting the data collection method is the amount of time participants must spend with data collection and evaluation systems. Time requirements should always be minimized, and the method should be positioned so that it is a value-added activity (that is, the participants understand that this activity is something valuable so they will not resist it). This requirement often means that sampling is used to keep the total participant time to a minimum. Some methods, such as performance monitoring, require no participant time, while others, such as interviews and focus groups, require a significant investment in time.

Cost of Method

Cost is always a consideration when selecting the method. Some data collection methods are more expensive than others. For example, interviews and observations are very expensive. Surveys, questionnaires, and performance monitoring are usually inexpensive.

Utility of an Additional Method (Source and Timeframe)

Because many different data collection methods exist, it is tempting to use too many methods. Multiple data collection methods add time and costs to the evaluation and may result in very little additional value. Utility refers to the added value of an additional data collection method. As more than one method is used, this question should always be addressed: Does the value obtained from the additional data warrant the extra time and expense of the method? If the answer is no, the additional method should not be implemented. The same issue must be addressed when considering multiple sources and timeframes.

Cultural Bias for Data Collection Method

The culture or philosophy of the organization can dictate which data collection methods are used. For example, some organizations or audiences are accustomed to using questionnaires because they work well within the culture. Some organizations will not use observation because their culture does not support the potential invasion of privacy associated with it.

Management's Time for Data Input

The time that a group member's immediate manager must allocate to data collection is another important issue when selecting a data collection method. Always strive to keep the managers' time requirements to a minimum. Some methods, such as focus groups, may require involvement from the manager prior to and after the intervention. Other methods, such as performance monitoring, may not require any manager time.

Disruption of Normal Work Activities

Another important factor in data collection is the amount of disruption created by the method selected. Routine work processes should be disrupted as little as possible. Some data collection techniques, such as business or operational databases, require little time or distraction from normal activities. Questionnaires generally do not disrupt the work environment and can often be completed in only a few minutes or even after normal work hours. Techniques such as focus groups and interviews may take more time for those involved.

Accuracy of Method

Accuracy is a factor to weigh when selecting a data collection method. Accuracy refers to the instrument's or the method's ability to correctly capture the data desired with minimum error. Some data collection methods are more accurate than others. For example, organization databases tend to be more accurate than an interview. If data are needed regarding on-the-job behavior, unobtrusive observation is a powerful option.

FINAL THOUGHTS

This chapter provided an overview of data collection methods that can be used in ROI analysis. Employee engagement practitioners and evaluators have the option to select from a variety of methods according to their resources, culture, and circumstances. Follow-up questionnaires and surveys are commonly used to collect data for application and impact analyses. Questionnaire design and ways to boost response rates were also explored. In the employee engagement field, the use of action plans and performance agreements can be very effective. Next up, data analysis . . . after the data are collected, what do you do with them?

5

Practical and Credible Data Analysis

Most employee engagement practitioners will agree that data analysis and interpretation is one of the most challenging tasks of measurement and evaluation. A misunderstanding of the techniques as well as a fear of math and statistics compound this challenge. This chapter describes five key steps in simple terms.

The first step is to isolate the impact of an employee engagement program, because other variables often influence the impact of an employee engagement program and these factors must be taken into account. The second step is to convert data to monetary values—it is one thing to collect the data, but assigning a monetary value to the data is a different process. The third step is to examine the costs of the program and the key elements to include when calculating them. The fourth step focuses on calculating the ROI and common approaches to calculate values that can be used in comparison with other types of investment. The final step is to discuss intangibles, which are the impact measures that are not converted to money. Refer back to Exhibit 2-2 for a visual depiction of the steps.

ISOLATING THE EFFECTS OF THE PROGRAM

The situation is not uncommon. An improvement in productivity is noted after a major employee engagement program has been implemented. The two events appear to be related, and an executive wants to know how much of the improvement was due to the employee engagement program. While this question is often asked, it is rarely answered with any degree of certainty. The change in performance may be related to the employee engagement program, but other factors may have also contributed because the employee engagement program was only one of many variables that may have influenced performance. This section explores several techniques that can be used to answer the question, "What impact did the employee engagement program have on performance?" with a much greater degree of certainty. Taking the time to carry out this step creates additional credibility for the process by focusing attention on other variables that may have influenced performance.

Use of Control Groups

The most credible approach for isolating the impact of an employee engagement program is to use control groups, similar to the way an experimental design process works. This approach involves an experimental group that has the benefit of the employee engagement program and a control group that does not. Both groups should have similar characteristics and, if feasible, be selected randomly. When this is possible, and both groups are subjected to the same environmental influences, the difference in each group's performance can be attributed to the employee engagement program. Exhibit 5-1 illustrates how the control group is set up. See the Case in Point sidebar for an example of using a control group in an employee engagement program.

Exhibit 5-1. Use of Control Groups

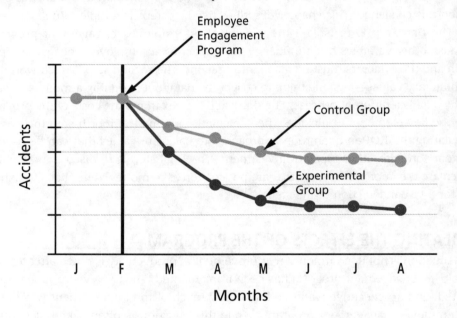

The use of control group arrangements has been around for a very long time. There is the story from biblical times in the Book of Daniel, dating back to 600 B.C. Daniel and his friends from Judah did not want to eat what the Babylonian royal court officials ate, so he proposed that he and his friends would eat vegetables and water for 10 days. When the 10 days were up, officials compared Daniel's group with the group that ate the royal food and found a significant difference in energy and health.

One major disadvantage of this method is that the program is withheld from one group. For example, take a situation in which the group that participated in an employee engagement study had $6 million more in revenue than the control group. Are the data gained from keeping the control group from the benefits of the program worth it? There always needs to be a solid business reason for using a control group.

Case in Point

A study focused on store employees who participated in a major employee engagement program. The participants' performance and business impact metrics were compared with that of a control group of an approximately equivalent number of stores with similar characteristics. Performance and business measures were tracked for the two groups for nine months in categories of sales, product returns, customer complaints, and turnover. The group that participated in the employee engagement program had significantly more positive outcomes than the control group. When study leaders converted sales, product returns, customer complaints, and turnover to monetary value using internal standards, the results showed an impressive ROI.

Trend Line Analysis

Another useful technique for approximating the impact of employee engagement programs is the trend line analysis. In this approach, a trend line is drawn on a graph from a point that represents the initial performance level of the target audience, and extends to a point that represents the anticipated performance level without the employee engagement program. Upon completion of the program, the actual performance is compared with the predicted performance level without the employee engagement program using the trend line. Any improvement in performance above what was predicted can be reasonably attributed to the employee engagement program. While this is not an exact process, it provides a reasonable estimation of the impact of an employee engagement program.

Exhibit 5-2 shows an example of a trend line analysis taken from a logistics company. The data are slightly exaggerated to illustrate the process. The exhibit shows the percentage of on-time shipments before and after an employee engagement program that was conducted in June. There was an established downward trend in the shipment rate prior to conducting the engagement program. The trend line shows that while this downward trend would have continued without the program, the employee engagement program had a dramatic effect on the on-time shipments. It is tempting to measure the improvement by comparing the average six-month shipping rates prior to the program with the average of the six months after the employee engagement program. However, a more accurate comparison is to compare the rate in month six after the program with the predicted trend line value of the same month. In this example, the difference is 27 percent (95 to 68).

Exhibit 5-2. Trend Line Analysis

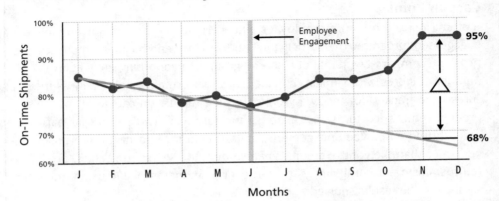

The main disadvantage of this approach is that it is not necessarily accurate, although it may be as accurate as other methods described in this chapter. This approach also assumes that the events influencing the performance variable prior to the program are still in place after the program and that no new influences entered the situation, with the exception of the implementation of the employee engagement program. The trends established prior to the program would have continued in the same relative direction without the program's influence. This may not always be the case.

The primary advantage of this approach is that it is simple and inexpensive, and it takes very little effort. If historical data are available, a trend line can quickly be drawn and data estimated. While this process is not exact, it does provide a quick analysis of the program's impact.

Forecasting Methods

A more analytical approach to trend line analysis is to use forecasting methods to predict the level of performance that might occur in the future if the employee engagement program is not implemented. This approach represents a mathematical interpretation of the trend line analysis, which uses a linear equation to calculate the value of the anticipated performance improvement. A linear model is only appropriate when one other variable influenced the output performance.

The primary advantage of this process is that it can be an accurate predictor of the performance variables that would occur without implementing the employee engagement program if appropriate data and models are available. The method is simple for linear relationships.

However, a major disadvantage to this approach occurs when many variables have to be considered, because the process becomes more complex and requires the use of a more sophisticated statistical analysis. Even then, the data may not fit the model. Unfortunately, many organizations have not developed mathematical relation-ships for output variables as a function of one or more inputs. Without them, the forecasting method is difficult to use. If the numbers are available, they could provide useful evidence of the impact of employee engagement. The presentation of specific methods is beyond the scope of this book and is contained in other works (Phillips and Phillips 2015).

Participant Estimation

An easy method to isolate the impact of an employee engagement program is to secure information directly from participants. This approach assumes that participants are capable of determining or estimating what portion of their performance improve-ment is related to the employee engagement program. Although their input is an estimate, it usually has considerable credibility with management groups because par-ticipants are at the center of the change or improvement resulting from the employee engagement program.

As an added enhancement, management may be asked to approve the partici-pants' estimates. For example, in an employee engagement program, participants were asked to estimate the amount of savings attributed to the engagement program. Then managers at the next two levels above those participating reviewed and approved the estimates. In essence, this means that the managers confirmed participants' esti-mates. Exhibit 5-3 shows a sample of these estimates.

Exhibit 5-3. Example of a Team Member's Estimates

Factor That Influenced Improvement	% of Improvement Caused by	Confidence Expressed as a %	Adjusted % of Improvement Caused by
EE Program	50%	87%	44%
Six Sigma	23%	83%	19%
Environmental Change	14%	62%	9%
System Change	13%	75%	10%
Other	__%	__%	__%
Total	100%		

The process has some disadvantages. Because it is an estimate, it does not have the accuracy desired by some professionals. In addition, the input data may be unreli-able if individuals are uncomfortable providing these types of estimates.

However, the approach also has several advantages. It is a simple process that is easily understood by participants and others who review evaluation data. There is also an extensive body of research that suggests these estimates are accurate; there is wis-dom in the crowds. This approach is inexpensive, takes little time and analysis, and results in an efficient addition to the evaluation process. Despite being an estimate, it originates from a credible source: the individuals who actually produced the improvement.

Manager's Estimation

In some cases, upper management may estimate the percent of improvement attributed to the employee engagement program. Although the process is subjective, the source of the estimate is a group that usually allocates funds and has a sense of what the value should be. With this approach, the source of these estimates is not usually based on direct knowledge of the process.

Expert Estimation

Another approach is to rely on external or internal experts to estimate what portion of results can be attributed to an employee engagement program. With this process, the experts must be carefully selected based on their knowledge of the process, intervention, and situation. For example, a company could ask an expert in quality to estimate how much quality improvement could be attributed to an employee engagement program and what percent should be attributed to other factors. In another situation, a company could ask an external expert to estimate the extent to which an improvement would be made without the engagement program. This amount would then be subtracted from the improvement, with the remainder assumed to be attributed to the employee engagement program. This approach is most effective when the expert has been involved in similar programs and is thus able to estimate the impact of those factors based on previous experience or historical data.

CONVERTING DATA TO MONETARY UNITS

Chapter 4 presented the types of data collected for employee engagement program evaluation. Before these data can be used to compare benefits with costs, they must be converted to monetary values. This section provides additional insight into practical ways to convert data to monetary values.

Converting Increased Output

Changes in output are the goal of many employee engagement programs, and in most situations the value of increased output can be easily calculated. For example, when implementing a program to increase sales, the change in output can easily be measured. Calculate the sales improvement after the program by multiplying it by the average profit per sale. In another example, consider packaging-machine operators in a pharmaceutical plant who package drugs for shipment. Production managers participate in a program to learn how to increase production through better use of equipment and work procedures. The value of the increased output is the operating profit margin. Fortunately, most of these conversions have been developed as standard values.

Converting Time Savings

Some employee engagement programs are aimed at reducing the time it takes to perform a task, deliver a service, or respond to a request. Time savings are important because employee time is money, as reflected in the form of wages, salaries, and paid benefits. The most common time savings result is reduced costs of effort for those involved in the employee engagement program. The monetary savings are the hours saved multiplied by the effort cost per hour.

Converting Improved Quality

Quality improvement is an important and frequent target of employee engagement programs. The cost of poor quality to an organization can be astounding. According to the late quality expert Phillip Crosby, an organization could increase its profits by 5 to 10 percent of sales if it concentrates on improving quality. To be effective, the measurable impact of an employee engagement program must be determined. To calculate the return on the program, the value of the quality improvement must be calculated.

The most obvious cost of poor quality is the scrap or waste generated by mistakes. Defective products, spoiled raw materials, and discarded paperwork are the results of poor quality. This scrap and waste translates into a monetary value that can be used to calculate the impact of an improvement in quality. The cost of a defective product can be easily calculated in a production environment; it is the total cost incurred at the point the mistake is identified minus the salvage value. The costs of paper and computer entry errors can also be significant; an error on a purchase order can be enormous if the wrong items are ordered.

Many mistakes and errors result in costly rework, especially when a product is delivered to a customer but must be returned for correction, or when an expensive product is implemented with serious errors. When determining the cost of rework, labor and direct cost are both significant. Maintaining a staff to perform rework is an additional overhead cost for the organization. In a manufacturing plant, for example, the cost of rework is in the range of 15 to 70 percent of a plant's productivity. In banks, an estimated 35 percent of operating costs could be blamed on correcting errors.

Using Historical Costs

Occasionally an organization will develop and accumulate cost for specific data items. For example, some organizations monitor the cost of grievances. Although it's extremely variable, the average cost per grievance provides a basis for estimating the cost savings for a reduction in grievances. Because of their relative accuracy, historical costs, if available, should be used to estimate the value of data items unless it takes too many resources.

Using Expert Input

Expert input, either internal or external, is sometimes used to estimate the value of soft data improvements. Internal experts are those employees who are proficient and knowledgeable in their fields. For example, a purchasing expert may estimate the salvage value of defective parts, an industrial engineer might estimate the time that it takes to complete a task or perform a function, and a marketing analyst might estimate the cost of a dissatisfied customer. Using internal experts provides excellent opportunities to recognize individuals in the organization. Their expert analysis should not be challenged because others in the organization have no better basis to make the estimate. External experts may also provide an estimate, depending on their expertise in a given field. One consultant may estimate the cost of work slowdowns and then use that figure with several organizations to provide an expert opinion.

EXTERNAL STUDIES

Extensive analyses of similar data in other organizations may be extrapolated to fit an internal situation. For example, many experts have attempted to calculate the cost of absenteeism. Although these estimates can vary considerably, they may still serve as a rough estimate for other calculations after some adjustments for the specific organization. There are hundreds of studies covering the cost of variables such as absenteeism, turnover, tardiness, grievances, complaints, and lost time due to accidents. Typical sources to pursue may include *Corporate Leadership Council, Academy of Management Journal, Journal of Applied Psychology, Personnel Psychology, Human Resources Management Review, OD Practitioner, Human Resource Development Quarterly,* and *Personnel Journal.*

However, practitioners rarely venture into external studies, probably because there is not enough dialogue between the practitioners and the researchers. Each group seems to have a misunderstanding of the other's role, and they only mesh at times when it is convenient for both. If practitioners learned more about research studies and publications, they might even be able to influence future research.

Participant Estimation

Employees that are directly involved in an employee engagement program may be capable of estimating the value of an improvement. Either during the employee engagement program or in a follow-up, participants should be asked to estimate the value of the improvements. To provide further insight, they should also be asked to furnish the basis for their estimate and their level of confidence in it. Estimations by participants are credible and may be more realistic than other sources because participants are usually directly involved with the improvement and are knowledgeable of the issues. If given encouragement and examples, participants are often creative at estimating these values. For example, asking managers to estimate the value of reducing the time to process a loan after participating in a special program. Although their responses won't be precise, they do provide a credible estimate of the value.

Management Estimation

A final strategy for converting soft data to monetary values is to ask managers who are concerned about the intervention's evaluation to estimate the value of an improvement. Several management groups may be targets for this estimation, including supervisors of employee engagement program participants, middle management, or even the C-suite.

These strategies are effective for converting soft data to monetary values when calculating the return on an employee engagement program. One word of caution is in order. Whenever a monetary value is assigned to subjective information, it needs to be fully explained to the audience receiving the information. When there is a range of possible values, the most conservative one should be used to ensure credibility for the process.

TABULATING THE COSTS OF THE PROGRAM

After an analysis yields a need, the organization designs and develops a solution or acquires one and implements it. The employee engagement team routinely reports to the client or sponsor throughout the process and then undertakes an evaluation to show the program's success. A group of costs also supports the process (such as administrative support and overhead costs). For costs to be fully understood, the project needs to be analyzed in several different categories.

The most important task is to define which specific costs are included in a tabulation of program costs. This step involves decisions that will be made by the employee engagement team and, in most cases, approved by management. If appropriate, finance and accounting staff may need to approve the list. Exhibit 5-4 shows the recommended cost categories for a fully loaded, conservative approach to estimating costs.

Needs Assessment Costs

One of the most overlooked cost items is the cost of conducting the initial assessment or diagnosis of the need for the employee engagement program. In some projects, this cost is zero because the program is implemented without an initial assessment of need. However, as organizations focus increased attention on needs assessment, this cost item becomes more significant.

Exhibit 5-4. Project Cost Categories

	Cost Item	Prorated	Expensed
1	**Needs assessment**	✔	
2	**Design and development**	✔	
3	**Acquisition costs**	✔	
4	**Implementation costs**		
	Salaries and benefits for coordination time		✔
	Salaries and benefits for participant time		✔
	Materials and supplies		✔
	Travel, lodging, and meals		✔
	Use of facilities		✔
	Capital expenditures		✔
5	**Maintenance and monitoring**		✔
6	**Administrative support and overhead**	✔	
7	**Evaluation and reporting**		✔

While it's best to collect data on all costs associated with the needs assessment to the fullest extent possible, estimates are appropriate. These costs include the time it takes team members to conduct the assessment, direct fees, expenses for external consultants who conduct the diagnosis, and internal services and supplies used in the analysis. The total costs are usually prorated over the life of the project. Depending on the type and nature of the project, the life cycle should be kept to a reasonable number in the one- to two-year timeframe. The exception would be for expensive projects for which the needs are not expected to change significantly for several years.

Design and Development Costs

One of the most significant items is the cost of developing the program. This cost item includes internal staff and consultant time for development of software, job aids, and other support material directly related to the project. As with diagnostics costs, development costs are usually prorated, perhaps using the same timeframe. Three to five years is recommended unless the project is expected to remain unchanged for many years and the development costs are significant.

Acquisition Costs

In lieu of development costs, many organizations purchase software or programs to use off the shelf or in a modified format. The acquisition costs for these programs include the purchase price and other costs associated with the rights to implement the program. These acquisition costs should be prorated, typically over three or five years, using the same rationale described previously. If the organization needs to modify or further develop the program, those costs should be included as development costs. In practice, many programs have both acquisition costs and development costs.

Implementation Costs

Perhaps the most important segment of employee engagement costs is implementation. Five major categories are included:

- Salaries of coordinators and organizers. The salaries of all individuals involved in coordination and direct support should be included. If a coordinator is involved in more than one program, the time should be allocated to the specific program under review. The key point is to account for all the direct time of internal employees or external consultants who work with the program. Include the employee benefits factor each time direct labor costs are involved.
- Materials and supplies. Specific project materials such as workbooks, handouts, brochures, guides, job aids, and iPads should be included in the delivery costs, along with any license fees, user fees, and royalty payments.
- Travel expenses. Include direct costs of travel, if required, for participants, facilitators, and coordinators. Lodging, meals, and other expenses also fall under this category.
- Facilities for sessions. Take into account the direct cost of the meeting facilities. When external meetings are held, this item represents the direct charge from the conference center or hotel. If meetings are held internally, use of the meeting room represents a cost to the organization and should be included, even if it is not the practice to include facility costs in other cost reporting.
- Participants' salaries and benefits. The salaries plus employee benefits of group members for their time away from work represent an expense that should be included. Estimates are appropriate in this analysis.

Maintenance and Monitoring

This item includes all costs related to routine operation of the program. It encompasses all costs in the same categories listed under implementation, plus perhaps equipment and services.

Overhead

Another charge is the cost of overhead, which is the additional costs of the employee engagement function that are not directly charged to a particular program. The overhead category represents any cost not considered in the previous calculations, such as the cost of administrative support, administrative expenses, salaries of employee engagement managers, and other fixed costs. A rough estimate developed through some type of allocation plan is usually sufficient.

Evaluation

The evaluation cost is included in the program costs to compute the fully loaded cost. For an ROI evaluation, the costs include developing the evaluation strategy and plans, designing instruments, collecting data, analyzing data, and preparing and presenting results. Cost categories include time, purchased services, materials, purchased instruments, and surveys.

CALCULATING THE RETURN ON INVESTMENT

The return on investment is an intriguing and important calculation. It is a figure that must be used with caution and care because it can be interpreted or misinterpreted in many ways. This section presents some general guidelines to help calculate the return and interpret its meaning.

Defining the Return on Investment

The term *return on investment* may appear to be out of place in employee engagement. The expression originates from finance and accounting and usually refers to the pretax contribution measured against controllable assets. It measures the anticipated profitability of an investment and is used as a standard measure of the performance of divisions and profit centers within a business.

A group of employees is often involved in an employee engagement program, so the investment figure should be the total costs of analysis, development, implementation, operating, and evaluation lumped together to form the bottom part of the equation. With these considerations for calculating the return on investment the following formula is used:

$$\text{ROI} = \frac{\text{Net Benefits}}{\text{Program Costs}} \times 100$$

The formula is multiplied by 100 to convert it to a percent. The net benefits are the benefits minus the costs.

To illustrate this calculation, consider an employee engagement program designed to reduce error rates. The average daily error rate per employee dropped from 20 to 15 because of the program. Before the program, an employee spent an average of 30 minutes correcting errors. If employees average $20 per hour and 20 employees completed the program, the weekly operational savings for this program using base pay savings is $1,000 (or 5 × 0.5 × $20 × 20). The annual savings are $52,000. If the program costs $40,000, the return on investment after the first year is:

$$\text{ROI} = \frac{\$52,000 - \$40,000}{\$40,000} \times 100 = 30 \text{ percent}$$

These figures may be more meaningful to managers who use ROI calculations for capital expenditures. ROI may be calculated prior to a program to estimate the potential cost effectiveness or after a program to measure the results achieved. The methods of calculation are the same.

Benefit-Cost Ratio

Another method for evaluating the investment is the benefit-cost ratio. Similar to the ROI, this ratio consists of the total of the benefits derived from the program expressed in monetary units, divided by the total cost of the program. A benefit-cost ratio greater than one indicates a positive return. A ratio of less than one indicates a loss. The benefits portion of the ratio is a tabulation of all the benefits derived from the program converted to monetary values and the total costs include all the cost categories, as described earlier in this chapter.

An advantage of the benefit-cost ratio is that it isn't linked to standard accounting procedures. Although the benefits are converted to monetary values, it is better to steer clear of standard accounting terminology because accounting measures can communicate a preciseness that is not always available when calculating the benefits or the cost portion of the equation.

Payback Period

A payback period is another method for evaluating a major expenditure. With this approach, the annual cash proceeds (savings) produced by investment are equated to the original cash outlay required by the investment to arrive at some multiple of cash proceeds equal to the original investment. Measurement is usually in terms of years and months. If the cost savings generated from a program are constant each year, the payback period is determined by dividing the total original cash investment (development costs, outside program purchase, and so on) by the amount of the expected annual savings. The savings that represent the net expenses are subtracted.

For example, if the program costs are $40,000, with a three-year useful life, and the benefits from the program are expected to be $52,000, then:

$$\text{Payback Period} = \frac{\text{Program Costs}}{\text{Annual Net Benefits}} \times 12 = \frac{\$40,000}{\$52,000} \times 12 = 9.23 \text{ months}$$

The program will "pay back" the original investment in 9.2 months. The payback period is simple to use but has the limitation of ignoring the time value of money.

IDENTIFYING THE INTANGIBLES

Perhaps the first step to understanding intangibles is to clearly define the difference between tangible and intangible assets in a business organization. As shown in Exhibit 5-5, tangible assets are required for business operations; they are readily visible, rigorously quantified, and routinely represented as line items on balance sheets. Intangible assets are the key to competitive advantage. They are invisible, difficult to quantify, and not tracked through traditional accounting practices. With this distinction, it is easy to understand why intangible measures are more challenging to convert to money. This next section will highlight a few intangible measures that are relevant for employee engagement.

EXHIBIT 5-5. Comparison of Tangible and Intangible Assets

Tangible Assets (Required for Business Operations)	Intangible Assets (Key to Competitive Advantage in Knowledge)
Readily visible	Invisible
Rigorously quantified	Difficult to quantify
Part of the balance sheet	Not tracked through accounting practices
Investment produces known returns	Assessment based on assumptions
Can be easily duplicated	Cannot be bought or imitated
Depreciates with use	Appreciates with purposeful use
Has finite application	Multiapplication without reducing value
Best managed with "scarcity" mentality	Best managed with abundance mentality
Best leveraged through control	Best leveraged through alignment
Can be accumulated	Dynamic—short shelf life when not in use

Culture and Climate

Organization culture is a very important factor for employee engagement, and various programs attempt to strengthen, solidify, or adjust the culture. Some organizations have a culture that is distinct and defined, but it can be a challenge to measure precisely.

It is possible to measure improvement using culture instruments to collect data before and after a program. The scores on these instruments represent important data that may be connected directly to the program. However, it is challenging to convert culture data to monetary value in practice; therefore, culture change may be listed as an intangible measure.

Some organizations conduct climate surveys, which reflect work climate changes such as communication, openness, trust, and quality of feedback. Closely related to organizational commitment and culture, climate surveys are very general and often focus on a range of workplace issues and environmental enablers and inhibitors. Climate surveys conducted before and after an employee engagement program is implemented may reflect the extent to which the program has changed these measures.

Diversity and Inclusion

Diversity and inclusion continues to be important as organizations strive to develop and nurture a diverse workforce. Engagement programs influence the diversity mix of the organization, and various data are available to measure the impact of focusing on diversity. The diversity mix is a measure showing employee categories along diversity definitions such as race, creed, color, national origin, age, religion, and sex. This diversity mix shows the makeup of the team at any given time and is not a measure that can be credibly converted to monetary value.

The payoff of having a diverse group influences several other measures, including absenteeism, turnover, discrimination complaints, morale, and sometimes productivity and quality. Many diversity perception instruments are available to measure the attitudes of employees toward diversity issues, and these are often administered before and after diversity projects. In addition, some organizations collect input on diversity issues in an annual feedback survey. All of these measures are important and reveal progress on an important issue, but they are difficult to convert directly to monetary value and are usually listed as intangibles.

Stress Reduction

Employee engagement programs can reduce work-related stress by preparing employees to identify and confront stress factors to improve job performance, accomplish more in a workday, and relieve tension and anxiety. The subsequent reduction in stress may be directly linked to the intervention. Although excessive stress may be directly linked to other, easy-to-convert data, such as productivity, absenteeism, and medical claims, it is usually listed as an intangible benefit.

FINAL THOUGHTS

This chapter discussed key issues in calculating the employee engagement contribution. The first and one of the most critical is the concept of isolating the employee engagement program, which determines the extent to which the improvement was caused by the program. The second issue involves converting data to monetary values. Regardless of the type of data, there are a number of strategies that can be extremely helpful in translating the data to monetary values to use in ROI formulas. The third aspect is the cost of the program. Calculating the return on investment is the fourth factor of data analysis, and there are several credible methods to do so. Finally, the ways to measure intangibles were addressed.

Data collection and analysis have little use without conveying the results to the right audience in the right way. The next chapter will highlight how to communicate the results.

REFERENCE

Phillips, P.P., and J.J. Phillips. 2015. *Making Human Capital Analytics Work: Measuring the ROI of Human Capital Processes and Outcomes*. New York: McGraw-Hill.

6

Reporting Results to Appropriate Audiences

A company implemented an employee engagement program to improve quality and speed of service. When the project ended the team measured the results, which were a mixed bag. The quality of service had improved, but the speed of service had not; in fact, it was slower than before. To share their findings, the team generated a report, which included major findings and charts and graphs, and distributed it to the executive team in an email. Unfortunately, the report was overlooked in the sea of emails received by the executive team. It wasn't until a face-to-face meeting on another topic that one member of the executive team commented on the mixed results and raised a lot of questions. The tone of the meeting became tense and uncomfortable. The HR executive remarked to her team afterward, "If I had to do it again, I would have escalated the need to communicate these findings in a different way."

The issues raised by this scenario help to illustrate common challenges of communicating findings—from reports with personal agendas to dealing with stakeholders who don't know their data and evaluation needs to groups who seemingly hide their findings under a rock.

You need to be able to answer several questions before you share your evaluation results: What and when is the best way to convey results? What is the purpose for the communication? Who is the intended audience? This chapter is about the final step in the ROI process, and will address these questions and more. It highlights the dos and don'ts of communicating evaluation findings, describes a best practice report formula that can be repeatedly used to sustain momentum and change, and outlines key ingredients for a communication plan.

GUIDELINES FOR COMMUNICATING RESULTS

Communicating results effectively is a systematic process with specific rules and steps. Here are seven guidelines.

Communicate Timely

Project results should usually be communicated as soon as they are known and packaged for presentation. As in the opening story, the timing of communication was a critical factor in the project. Not sharing the results in a timely fashion led to a missed opportunity for well-timed improvement. Several questions about timing must be addressed:

- Is the audience prepared for the information when considering the content and other events?
- Are they expecting it?
- When is the best time to have the maximum impact on the audience?

Customize Your Communication to a Specific Audience

The communication will be more efficient when it is designed for a specific group. The message can be specifically tailored to the interests, needs, and expectations of the group. The length, content, detail, and slant will vary with the audience. Exhibit 6-1 shows the specific audience groups with the most common reasons for communicating results.

Exhibit 6-1. Common Target Audiences

Primary Target Audience	Reason for Communication
Client	To secure approval results
All managers	To gain support for employee engagement
Participants	To secure agreement with the issues, create the desire to be involved, and improve the results and quality of the data
Top executives	To enhance the credibility of the employee engagement team
Immediate managers	To reinforce the processes and build support for the program
Employee engagement team	To drive action for improvement
Facilitators	To prepare participants for the program
Human resources	To show the complete results of the program
Evaluation team	To underscore the importance of measuring results
All employees	To demonstrate accountability for expenditures
Prospective clients	To market future programs

The most important target audience is probably the client; this often involves senior management because they need information to approve funding. The entire management group may also need to be informed about project results in a general way. Management's support for, and involvement in, employee engagement is important to the success of the effort. The department's credibility is another key issue, and communicating project results to management can help establish this credibility.

The importance of communicating with a participant's immediate manager is probably obvious, as these managers may need to support and allow employees to be involved in programs. An adequate return on investment improves their commitment to employee engagement while enhancing the employee engagement team's credibility with them.

Participants also need feedback on the overall success of their efforts. However, this target audience is often overlooked under the assumption that they don't need to know about the overall success of the program.

The employee engagement team members should also receive information about program results, and depending on the team's reporting relationships, HR may be included too. For small teams, the individual conducting the evaluation may be the same person who coordinated the effort. For larger departments the evaluation may be done by a separate function. In either case, the team needs detailed information about the program's effectiveness so that adjustments can be made if the project is repeated.

Select the Mode of Communication Carefully

Depending on the group, one medium may be more effective than others, so it is important to select the appropriate medium to communicate the results. For example, face-to-face meetings may be better than special reports for some groups, whereas a brief summary to senior management will likely be more effective than a full-blown evaluation report. Exhibit 6-2 illustrates options for communicating results.

Exhibit 6-2. Options for Communicating Results

Detailed Reports	Brief Reports	Electronic Reporting	Mass Publications
Impact study	Executive summary	Website	Announcements
Case study (internal)	Slide overview	Email	Bulletins
Case study (external)	One-page summary	Blog	Newsletters
Major articles	Brochure	Video	Brief articles

Keep Communication Neutral

The challenge for the evaluator is to remain neutral and unbiased. Let the results inform as to whether the program hit the mark. Separate facts from fiction, and replace opinions with data-driven statements. Some target audiences may view communication from the employee engagement team with skepticism and may look for biased information and opinions. Boastful statements may turn off individuals, and then most of the content of the communication will be lost. Observable, believable facts carry more weight than extreme claims.

Include Testimonials

Testimonials are more effective if they are from individuals with audience credibility. Perceptions are strongly influenced by others, particularly by those who are admired or respected. Testimonials about employee engagement program results, when solicited from individuals who are generally respected in the organization, can have a strong impact on the effectiveness of the message. They can usually be collected from participants at each level: reaction, learning, application, and impact.

Be Consistent

Look for ways to include evaluation reporting, using the timing and forums of other organization reports. The content of the communication should be consistent with organization practices. A special communication at an unusual time may create more work than it's worth. When a particular group, such as senior management, regularly receives communication, the information sharing should continue, even if the results are not what were desired. If some results (such as negative ones) are omitted, it might leave the impression that only good results are reported.

Use Communication to Drive Improvement

Because information is collected at different points during the process, providing feedback to the groups enables them to take action and make adjustments if needed. As a result, the quality and timeliness of communication is critical to making improvements. Even after the evaluation is completed, communication is necessary to make sure the target audience fully understands the results achieved, as well as how the results may be enhanced in future programs or in the current program, if it is still operational. Communication is the key to making important adjustments at all phases of the project.

THE CAUTIONS OF COMMUNICATING RESULTS

Communications can go astray or miss the mark. Several cautions should be observed early and often in the process. Here are four critical ones.

Don't Hide the Results

The least desired communication action is doing nothing. Communicating results is almost as important as producing results. Getting results without communicating them is like planting a flower and not watering it. By not sharing the findings from your project, the organization can miss out on a key opportunity to make adjustments and bring about the change that is desired.

Don't Overlook the Political Aspects of Communication

Communication is one of those issues that can cause major problems. Because the results of a program may be closely linked to political issues within an organization, communicating them can upset some individuals while pleasing others. If certain individuals do not receive the information, or if information is delivered inconsistently between groups, problems can quickly surface. The information must not only be understood, but issues relating to fairness, quality, and political correctness make it crucial that the communication be constructed and delivered effectively to all key individuals.

Don't Skimp on the Recommendations

Recommendations are probably one of the most critical issues—they are the main conduit to change. And yet they often seem to be given as a last-minute thought or skipped altogether. The best recommendations include specific action-oriented steps that come from the conclusions of the evaluation study and are then discussed with key stakeholders for buy-in and ownership. The point is to collaborate with stakeholders on this section so that the company can internalize the results and needed action.

Don't Ignore the Audience's Opinion

Opinions are difficult to change and a negative opinion toward a program or team may not change simply by presenting the facts. However, it may strengthen the opinions held by those who already support the program because it reinforces their position and provides a defense they can use in discussions with others. A project team with a high level of credibility and respect may have a relatively easy time communicating results. Low credibility can create problems when one is trying to be persuasive.

THE COMPLETE REPORT

The type of report to be issued depends on the degree of detail and the information presented to the various target audiences. Brief summaries of project results with appropriate charts may be sufficient for some communication efforts. In other situations, particularly those involving major projects requiring extensive funding, a detailed evaluation report is crucial. A complete and comprehensive impact study report is usually necessary at least in the early use of the ROI Methodology. This report can then be used as the basis for more streamlined information aimed at specific audiences using various media. The following report formula is one way to effectively convey the results. It has all the necessary ingredients to communicate outcomes in the best possible way.

- General Information
  - Background: What were the needs that precipitated the program? Why was this program selected?

- — Objectives of study: What are the goals and targets for this program? What are the intended results?
- Methodology for Impact Study
  - — Levels of evaluation: Describe the evaluation framework to set the stage for showing the results.
  - — ROI process: Briefly describe the 10-step process that was used.
  - — Collecting data: What methods were selected to collect data and why? Also, when were data collected?
  - — Isolating the effects of the program: What method was used to isolate the effects of the intervention and why?
  - — Converting data to monetary values: What methods were used to convert data to money?
- Data Analysis: How were data analyzed? What methods were used?
- Costs: Itemize the costs of the intervention.
- Results: General Information
- Response profile: Include demographics of the population that responded or participated in the evaluation. If a questionnaire was used, what was the return rate and the anticipated return rate?
- Results: Reaction and Planned Action
  - — Data sources
  - — Data summary
  - — Key issues
- Results: Learning
  - — Data sources
  - — Data summary
  - — Key issues
- Results: Application and Implementation
  - — Data sources
  - — Data summary
  - — Key issues
- Results: Impact
  - — Data sources
  - — Data summary
  - — Key issues
- Results: ROI Calculation and What It Means
- Results: Intangible Measures
- Barriers and Enablers: This section of the report can be a powerful mechanism to lead into conclusions and recommendations. What obstacles were experienced that kept the organization from experiencing the kind of results they wanted? If barriers were noted, this should turn into some action items for the organization.

- Conclusions: Summarize key findings from the data.
- Recommendations: Based on the conclusions, what type of action needs to take place? What are stakeholders willing to do?

While the impact study report is an effective, professional way to present ROI data, several cautions are in order. Because this report documents the success of a program involving other individuals, credit for the success must go completely to those involved—the organization members who participated in the program and their immediate leaders. Their performance generated the success.

The methodology should be clearly explained, along with the assumptions made in the analysis. The reader should easily see how the values were developed and how specific steps were followed to make the process more conservative, credible, and accurate. Detailed statistical analyses should be placed in an appendix.

USING MEETINGS

If used properly, meetings are fertile ground for communicating program results. All organizations hold a variety of meetings, and some may provide the proper context to convey program results. Along the chain of command, staff meetings are held to review progress, discuss current problems, and distribute information. These meetings can be an excellent forum for discussing the results achieved in a program that relates to the group's activities. Program results can also be sent to executives for use in a staff meeting, or a member of the evaluation team can attend the meeting to make a presentation.

Regular meetings with management groups are a common practice. Typically, discussions will focus on items that might be of help to work units. The discussion of a program and its results can be integrated into the regular meeting format. A few organizations have initiated the use of periodic meetings for all key stakeholders, where a project leader reviews progress and discusses next steps. A few highlights from interim program results can be helpful in building interest, commitment, and support for the program.

Presentation of Results to Senior Management

Perhaps one of the most challenging and stressful types of communication is presenting an impact study to the senior management team, which also serves as the client for a project. The challenge is convincing this highly skeptical and critical group that outstanding results have been achieved (assuming they have) in a very reasonable timeframe, addressing the salient points, and making sure the managers understand the process. Two potential reactions can create problems. First, if the results are very impressive, making the managers accept the data may be difficult. On the other extreme, if the data are negative, ensuring that managers don't overreact and look for someone to blame is important. Several guidelines can help ensure that this process is planned and executed properly.

ROUTINE COMMUNICATION TOOLS

An internal, routine publication—such as a newsletter, magazine, newspaper, or electronic message—is one way to reach all employees or stakeholders and share program results. The content can have a significant impact if it is communicated appropriately; however, the scope should be limited to general-interest articles, announcements, and interviews.

Results communicated through these types of media must be important enough to arouse general interest. For example, a story with the headline "New Employee Engagement Program Increases Profits" will catch the attention of many readers because they probably know about the program and can appreciate the relevance of the results. Reports on the accomplishments of a small group of organization members may not generate interest if the audience cannot relate to the accomplishments.

For many projects, results are not achieved until weeks or even months after the program is completed. Communicating results to a general audience may lead to motivation to continue the program or introduce similar ones in the future.

Stories about those involved in a program and the results they have achieved can help create a favorable image. Employees see that the organization is investing resources to improve performance and prepare for the future. This type of story provides information about a program that may otherwise be unknown, and sometimes creates a desire for others to participate. Public recognition of program participants who deliver exceptional performance can enhance employee engagement and drive them to excel.

ROUTINE FEEDBACK ON PROGRESS

A primary reason for collecting reaction and learning data is to provide feedback so that adjustments can be made throughout the program. For most programs, data are routinely collected and quickly communicated to a variety of groups. One method of doing this is to use a feedback action plan, which is designed to provide information to several audiences using a variety of media. These feedback sessions have the ability to point out specific actions that need to be taken, but they can become complex and so must be managed in a very proactive manner. The following steps are recommended for providing feedback and managing the overall process. Many of the steps and concepts are based on the recommendations of Peter Block in his landmark book, *Flawless Consulting*.

- **Communicate quickly.** Whether the news is good or bad, it should be passed on to individuals involved in the project as soon as possible. The recommended time for providing feedback is usually a matter of days, and certainly no longer than a week or two after the results become known.
- **Simplify the data.** Condense the data into an easily understandable, concise presentation. This is not the appropriate time to include detailed explanation and analysis.
- **Examine the role of the employee engagement team and the client in the feedback process.** The engagement team can wear many hats in the process. And sometimes the client plays roles that the team is used to filling. These respective functions must be examined in terms of reactions to the data and the recommended actions.
- **Use negative data in a constructive way.** Some of the data will show that things are not going so well, and the fault may rest with the project leader or the client. In this case, the story basically changes from "let's look at the success we've achieved," to "now we know which areas to change."
- **Use positive data in a cautious way.** Positive data can be misleading, and if they are communicated too enthusiastically, they may create expectations that exceed what finally materializes. Be cautious when presenting positive data and allow the response to be fully in the hands of the client.
- **Choose the language used in the meeting and the communication carefully.** The language used should be descriptive, focused, specific, short, and simple. Avoid any language that is too judgmental, full of jargon, stereotypical, lengthy, or complex.
- **Ask the client for reactions to the data.** After all, the client is the number 1 customer, and it is most important that the client be pleased with the project.
- **Ask the client for recommendations.** The client may have some good suggestions for what needs to be changed to keep a project on track, or to put it back on track should it derail.
- **Use support and confrontation carefully.** These two actions are not mutually exclusive. At times, both support and confrontation are needed for a particular group. The client may need support and yet be confronted for lack of improvement or sponsorship. The project team may be confronted regarding the problem areas that have developed, but may also need support.
- **Act on the data.** The different alternatives and possibilities should be weighed carefully to arrive at the necessary adjustments.
- **Secure agreement from all key stakeholders.** Agreement is essential to ensure that everyone is willing to make the suggested changes.

- **Keep the feedback process short.** Don't allow the process to become bogged down in long, drawn-out meetings or lengthy documents. If this occurs, stakeholders will avoid the process instead of being willing participants.

Following these steps will help move the project forward and generate useful feedback, often ensuring that adjustments are supported and can be executed.

THE COMMUNICATION PLAN

Any activity must be carefully planned to achieve maximum results. This is a critical part of communicating the results of the program. The actual planning of the communication is important to ensure that each audience receives the proper information at the right time and that necessary actions are taken. Several issues are crucial in planning the communication of results:

- What will be communicated?
- When will the data be communicated?
- How will the information be communicated?
- Where will the information be communicated?
- Who will communicate the information?
- Who is the target audience?
- What are the specific actions required or desired?

The communication plan is usually established when the program is approved. This plan details how specific information is developed and communicated to various groups, as well as the expected actions. In addition, it details how the overall results will be communicated, the timeframe for communication, and the appropriate groups to receive the information. The employee engagement team leader, key managers, and stakeholders will need to agree on the degree of detail in the plan.

FINAL THOUGHTS

The final step in the ROI Methodology, communication of results, is a crucial step in the overall evaluation process. If not executed adequately, the full impact of the results will not be recognized and the study may amount to a waste of time. This chapter began with general dos and don'ts for communicating results, which can serve as a guide for any significant communication effort. The various target audiences were then discussed, along with the most commonly used media for communicating project results. The next chapter will discuss how to sustain the momentum of evaluation and overcome barriers to using the methodology.

REFERENCE

Block, P. 2011. *Flawless Consulting: A Guide to Getting Your Expertise Used,* 3rd Ed. San Francisco: Pfeiffer.

Implementing and Sustaining ROI

E ven the best-designed process, model, or technique is worthless unless it is effectively and efficiently integrated into the organization. Change is not permanent for many reasons, one of which is resistance. As it relates to the use of the ROI Methodology, some of this resistance is based on fear and misunderstanding. Some is real, based on actual barriers and obstacles. Although the ROI process presented in this book is a step-by-step, methodical, and simplistic procedure, it can fail if it is not integrated properly, fully accepted, and supported by those who must make it work within the organization. This chapter focuses on some of the most effective means of overcoming resistance to implementing the ROI process in an organization.

THE IMPORTANCE OF SUSTAINING THE USE OF ROI

There is resistance with any new process or change. It may be especially great when implementing a process as complex as ROI. To implement ROI and sustain it as an important accountability tool, the resistance must be minimized or removed. Here are four reasons to have a plan.

Resistance is always present. Sometimes there are good reasons for resistance, but often it exists for the wrong reasons. It is important to sort out both kinds of resistance and try to dispel the myths. When legitimate barriers are the basis for resistance, the challenge is to minimize or remove them completely.

Implementation is key. As with any process, effective implementation is key to its success. This occurs when the new technique, tool, or process is integrated into the routine framework. Without effective implementation, even the best process will fail. A process that is never removed from the shelf will never be understood, supported, or improved. Clear-cut steps must be in place for designing a comprehensive implementation process that will overcome resistance.

Implementation requires consistency. Consistency is an important consideration as the ROI process is implemented. With consistency comes accuracy and reliability. The only way to make sure consistency is achieved is to follow clearly defined processes and procedures each time the ROI Methodology is used. Proper, effective implementation will ensure that this occurs.

Implementation requires efficiency. Cost control and efficiency will be significant considerations in any major undertaking, and the ROI Methodology is no exception. During implementation, tasks must be completed efficiently and effectively. Doing so will help ensure that process costs are kept to a minimum, that time is used economically, and that the process remains affordable.

IMPLEMENTING THE PROCESS: OVERCOMING RESISTANCE

Resistance shows up in a variety of ways, including comments, remarks, actions, or behaviors. The following is a list of comments that indicate an open resistance to the ROI process:

- It costs too much.
- It takes too much time.
- Who is asking for this?
- This is not in my job description.
- I did not have input on this.
- I do not understand this.
- What happens when the results are negative?
- How can we be consistent with this?
- The ROI looks too subjective.
- Our managers will not support this.
- ROI is too narrowly focused.
- This is not practical.

Each comment signals an issue that must be resolved or addressed in some way. A few are based on realistic barriers, whereas others are based on myths that must be dispelled. Resistance to the process may reflect underlying concerns. For example, owners of programs may fear losing control of the programs, while others may feel vulnerable to whatever actions may follow if the program is not successful. Still others may be concerned about any process that brings change or requires additional effort.

Practitioners may resist the ROI process and openly make comments similar to those listed, and it may take evidence of tangible and intangible benefits to convince them that it is in their best interest to make the project a success. Although most clients want to see the results of the program, they may have concerns about the information they are asked to provide and about whether their personal performance is being judged while the project is undergoing evaluation. Participants may express the same fears.

The challenge is to implement the methodology systematically and consistently so that it becomes normal business behavior and part of a routine and standard process built into projects. The implementation necessary to overcome resistance covers a variety of areas. Exhibit 7-1 shows the actions outlined in this chapter, which are presented as building blocks to overcoming resistance. They are all necessary to build the proper base or framework to dispel myths and remove or minimize barriers.

The remainder of this chapter presents specific strategies and techniques devoted to each building block. They apply equally to the employee engagement team and the client organization, and no attempt is made to separate the two.

EXHIBIT 7-1. Building Blocks for Overcoming Resistance

Monitoring Progress; Reporting Results
Removing Obstacles
Preparing the Management Team
Initiating the Projects
Preparing the Staff; Skill Development
Revising Policies, Procedures, and Practices
Establishing Goals and Plans for the Transition
Developing Roles and Responsibilities
Assessing the Status of Delivering Results

ASSESSING THE CLIMATE

As a first step toward implementation, some organizations assess the current climate for achieving results. One way to do this is to develop a survey to determine the current perspectives of the employee engagement team and other stakeholders. A special instrument is available for this at ROI Institute (www.roiinstitute.net). Another way is to conduct interviews with key stakeholders to determine their willingness to follow the program through to ROI. With an awareness of the current status, the employee engagement team can plan for significant changes and pinpoint particular issues that need support as the ROI process is implemented.

DEVELOPING ROLES AND RESPONSIBILITIES

Defining and detailing specific roles and responsibilities for different groups and individuals addresses many of the resistance factors and helps pave a smooth path for implementation.

Identifying a Champion

As an early step in the process, one or more individuals should be designated as the internal leader or champion for the ROI Methodology. As in most change efforts, someone must take responsibility for ensuring that the process is implemented successfully. This leader serves as a champion for ROI and is usually the one who understands the process best and sees vast potential for its contribution. More important, this leader is willing to teach others and will work to sustain sponsorship.

Develop the ROI Leader

In a project to improve employee engagement, the ROI leader is usually a member of the employee engagement team who has the responsibility for evaluation. For large organizations, the ROI leader may be part of HR. This person will either hold a full-time position on a larger program team or a part-time position on a smaller team. Client organizations may also have an ROI leader who pursues the ROI Methodology from the client's perspective. The typical job title for a full-time ROI leader is manager or director of analytics or measurement and evaluation. Some organizations assign this responsibility to a team and empower it to lead the ROI effort.

In preparation for this assignment, individuals usually receive special training that builds specific skills and knowledge of the ROI process. The role of the implementation leader is quite broad and serves many specialized duties. In some organizations, the implementation leader can take on many roles, ranging from diagnostician to problem solver to communicator.

Leading the ROI process is a difficult and challenging assignment that requires unique skills. Fortunately, programs that teach these skills are available. For example, ROI Institute offers a program that is designed to certify individuals who will be assuming leadership roles in the implementation of the ROI Methodology. This certification is built around 10 specific skill sets linked to successful ROI implementation, focusing on the critical areas of data collection, isolating the effects of the project, converting data to monetary value, presenting evaluation data, and building capability. This process is quite comprehensive but may be necessary to build the skills needed for taking on this challenging assignment.

Establishing a Task Force

Making the ROI Methodology work well may require the use of a task force. A task force usually comprises a group of individuals from different parts of the project or client team who are willing to develop the ROI Methodology and implement it in the organization. The selection of the task force may involve volunteers, or participation may be mandatory depending on specific job responsibilities. The task force should represent the cross section necessary for accomplishing any stated goals. Task forces have the additional advantage of bringing more people into the process and developing more ownership of and support for the ROI Methodology. The task force must be large enough to cover the key areas, but not so large that it becomes too cumbersome to function. Six to 12 members is a good size.

Assigning Responsibilities

Determining specific responsibilities is critical because confusion can arise when individuals are unclear about their specific assignments in the ROI process. Responsibilities apply to two areas. The first is the measurement and evaluation responsibility of the entire employee engagement team. Everyone involved in the program will have some responsibility for measurement and evaluation. These responsibilities may include providing input on designing instruments, planning specific evaluations, analyzing data, and interpreting the results. Typical responsibilities include:

- ensuring that the initial analysis or diagnosis for the project includes specific business impact measures
- developing specific application and business impact objectives for the project
- keeping the organization or team members focused on application and impact objectives
- communicating rationale and reasons for evaluation
- assisting in follow-up activities to capture application and business impact data
- providing assistance for data collection, data analysis, and reporting.

Although involving each member of the employee engagement team in all these activities may not be appropriate, each individual should have at least one responsibility as part of his routine job duties. This assignment of responsibility keeps the ROI Methodology from being disjointed and separated during projects. More important, it brings accountability to those directly involved in implementation.

The assignment of responsibilities for evaluation requires attention throughout the evaluation process. Although the team must be assigned specific responsibilities during an evaluation, requiring others to serve in support functions to help with data collection is not unusual. These responsibilities are defined when a particular evaluation strategy is developed and approved.

ESTABLISHING GOALS AND PLANS

Establishing goals, targets, and objectives is critical to the implementation, particularly when several evaluations are planned. The establishment of goals can include detailed planning documents for the overall process and for individual ROI projects.

Setting Evaluation Targets

Establishing specific targets for evaluation levels is an important way to make progress with measurement and evaluation. As emphasized throughout this book, not every program should be evaluated to the ROI level. Knowing in advance to which level the program will be evaluated helps in planning what measures will be needed and how detailed the evaluation must be at each level. Exhibit 7-2 presents an example of the targets set for evaluation at each level from one of the largest telecommunications companies in the world. Targets should be set early in the process, with the full support of the entire team. If practical and feasible, the targets should also have the approval of key managers—particularly the senior management team.

EXHIBIT 7-2. Evaluation Targets in a Large Organization

Level	Target*
Level 1, Reaction	100%
Level 2, Learning	80%
Level 3, Application and Implementation	30%
Level 4, Business Impact	10%
Level 5, ROI	5%

Percent of HR programs evaluated at this level.

Developing a Plan for Implementation

An important part of implementation is establishing a timetable for the complete implementation of the ROI process. This document becomes a master plan for completion of the different elements presented earlier. Beginning with forming a team and concluding with meeting the targets previously described, this schedule is a project plan for transitioning from the present situation to the desired future situation. Items on the schedule include developing specific ROI projects, building staff skills, developing policy, and teaching managers the process. Exhibit 7-3 shows an example of a plan for implementing ROI in HR for a large petroleum company. The more detailed the document, the more useful it becomes. The project plan is a living, long-range document that should be reviewed frequently and adjusted as necessary. More important, those engaged in work on the ROI Methodology should always be familiar with it.

REVISING OR DEVELOPING GUIDELINES AND PROCEDURES

Another part of planning is revising or developing the organization's policy or guidelines on measurement and evaluation. The guidelines document contains information developed specifically for the measurement and evaluation process. It is created with input from the team and key managers or stakeholders, and may be addressed during internal workshops designed to build measurement and evaluation skills. This statement addresses critical matters that will influence the effectiveness of the measurement and evaluation process. These may include adopting the five-level framework presented in this book, requiring Level 3 and 4 objectives for some or all programs, and defining responsibilities for the employee engagement team.

Exhibit 7-3. ROI Implementation Plan for a Large Petroleum Company

	J	F	M	A	M	J	J	A	S	O	N	D	J	F	M	A	M	J	J	A	S	O	N
Team formed	▓																						
Responsibilities defined		▓																					
Policy developed			▓	▓																			
Targets set		▓	▓																				
Workshops developed					▓	▓																	
ROI Project (A)								▓	▓														
ROI Project (B)							▓	▓					▓										
ROI Project (C)												▓	▓	▓									
ROI Project (D)														▓	▓	▓							
Project teams trained								▓												▓	▓		
Managers trained																		▓	▓	▓			
Support tools developed				▓	▓																		
Guidelines developed						▓																	

103

Guidelines are important because they provide structure and direction for the team and others who work closely with the ROI Methodology. These individuals keep the process clearly focused, and enable the group to establish goals for evaluation. Guidelines also provide an opportunity to communicate basic requirements and fundamentals of performance and accountability. More than anything, they serve as learning tools to teach others, especially when they are developed collaboratively. If guidelines are developed in isolation, the team and management will be denied their sense of ownership, rendering them neither effective nor useful.

Procedures for measurement and evaluation are important for showing how to use the tools and techniques, guide the design process, provide consistency in the ROI process, ensure that appropriate methods are used, and place the proper emphasis on each of the areas. The procedures are more technical than the guidelines and often include detailed steps showing how the process is undertaken and developed. They often include specific forms, instruments, and tools necessary to facilitate the process.

PREPARING THE TEAM

Employee engagement team members may see evaluation as an unnecessary intrusion into their responsibilities that absorbs precious time and stifles creative freedom. The cartoon character Pogo perhaps characterized it best when he said, "We have met the enemy, and he is us." Several issues must be addressed when preparing the employee engagement team for ROI implementation.

Involving the Employee Engagement Team

For each key issue or major decision regarding ROI implementation, involve the team in the process. As evaluation guidelines are prepared and procedures are developed, team input is essential. It will be more difficult for the team to resist if they helped design and develop the ROI process. Convene meetings, brainstorming sessions, and task forces to involve the team in every phase of developing the framework and supporting documents for ROI.

Using ROI as a Learning and Process Improvement Tool

One reason the employee engagement team may resist the ROI process is fear of failure, because the program's effectiveness will be fully exposed, putting the reputation of the team on the line. To overcome this, the ROI Methodology should be clearly positioned as a tool for learning and process improvement, not a tool for evaluating project team performance (at least not during the early years of project implementation). Team members will not be interested in developing a process that may reflect unfavorably on their performance.

Evaluators can learn as much from failures as from success. If the program is not working, it is best to find out quickly so that issues can be understood firsthand, not from others. If the program is ineffective and not producing the desired results, the failure will eventually be discovered by clients and the management group (if they are not aware of it already). A lack of results will make managers less supportive of immediate and future projects. If the weaknesses are identified and adjustments made quickly, not only can more effective projects be developed, but the credibility of and respect for project implementation can also be enhanced.

Teaching the Team

The employee engagement team usually has inadequate skills in measurement and evaluation, because these areas are not always a formal part of the team's or evaluator's job preparation. Consequently, the employee engagement team leader must learn ROI Methodology and its systematic steps; the evaluator must learn to develop an evaluation strategy and a specific plan to collect and analyze data from the evaluation and interpret results from data analysis.

INITIATING ROI STUDIES

The first tangible evidence of the value of using the ROI Methodology may be seen at the initiation of the first employee engagement program for which an ROI calculation is planned. Because of this, it is important to identify appropriate programs and keep them on track.

Selecting the Initial Project

It is critical that appropriate employee engagement programs be selected for ROI analysis. Only certain types of projects qualify for comprehensive, detailed analysis. The characteristics of programs that are suitable for analysis were presented in chapter 3.

Developing the Planning Documents

Perhaps the two most useful ROI documents are the data collection plan and the ROI analysis plan. The data collection plan shows what data will be collected, the methods used, the sources, the timing, and the assignment of responsibilities. The ROI analysis plan shows how specific analyses will be conducted, including how to isolate the effects of the project and how to convert data to monetary values. Each evaluator should know how to develop these plans. Please refer to chapter 4 for more details.

Status meetings should be conducted to report progress and discuss critical issues with appropriate team members. These meetings keep the employee engagement team focused on the critical issues, generate the best ideas for addressing problems and barriers, and build a knowledge base for better implementation of future evaluations. In essence, the meetings serve three major purposes: reporting progress, learning, and planning.

PREPARING THE CLIENTS AND EXECUTIVES

Perhaps no group is more important to the ROI process than the management team that must allocate resources for the employee engagement program and then support its implementation. In addition, the management team often provides input to and assistance for the ROI process. Preparing, training, and developing the management team should be carefully planned and executed.

One effective approach for preparing executives and managers for the ROI process is to conduct a briefing on ROI. Varying in duration from one hour to half a day, this type of practical briefing can provide critical information and enhance support for ROI use. Managers leave these briefings with greater appreciation of ROI and its potential impact on projects, as well as a clearer understanding of their role in the process. More important, they often renew their commitment to react to and use the data collected by the ROI Methodology.

A strong, dynamic relationship between the employee engagement team and key managers is essential for successful implementation of the ROI Methodology. There must be a productive partnership that requires each party to understand the concerns, problems, and opportunities of the other. Developing a beneficial relationship is a long-term process that must be deliberately planned for and initiated by key employee engagement team members. The decision to commit resources and support an intervention may be based on the effectiveness of this relationship.

REMOVING OBSTACLES

As the ROI Methodology is implemented, obstacles to its progress will inevitably crop up. The obstacles are based on concerns discussed in this chapter, some of which may be valid, others of which may be based on unrealistic fears or misunderstandings.

Dispelling Myths

As part of the implementation, attempts should be made to dispel the myths and remove or minimize the barriers or obstacles. Much of the controversy regarding ROI stems from misunderstandings about what the process can and cannot do, and how it can or should be implemented in an organization. Some of the biggest misunderstandings include:

- ROI is too complex for most users.
- ROI is expensive and consumes too many critical resources.
- If senior management does not require ROI, there is no need to pursue it.

- ROI is a passing fad.
- ROI is only one type of data.
- ROI is not future-oriented; it only reflects past performance.
- ROI is rarely used by organizations.
- The ROI Methodology cannot be easily replicated.
- ROI is not a credible process; it is too subjective.
- ROI cannot be used with soft projects.
- Isolating the influence of other factors is not always possible.
- ROI is only appropriate for large organizations.
- No standards exist for the ROI Methodology.

Delivering Bad News

One of the most difficult obstacles to overcome is receiving inadequate, insufficient, or disappointing news. The time to think about bad news is early in the process, but without losing sight of its value. In essence, bad news means that things can change, they need to change, and the situation can improve. The team simply needs to be convinced that good news can be found in a bad-news situation. Here is some advice to follow when delivering bad news:

- Never fail to recognize the power to learn and improve with a negative study.
- Look for red flags along the way.
- Lower outcome expectations with key stakeholders along the way.
- Look for data everywhere.
- Never alter the standards.
- Remain objective throughout the process.
- Prepare the team for the bad news.
- Consider different scenarios.
- Find out what went wrong.
- Adjust the story line to: "Now we have data that show how to make this program more successful." In an odd way, this puts a positive spin on data that are less than positive.

Using the Data

It is unfortunately too often the case that programs are evaluated and significant data are collected, but no action is taken. Failure to use data is a tremendous obstacle because the team has a tendency to move on to the next project or issue and focus on other priorities. Exhibit 7-4 shows how the different levels of data can be used to improve projects. It is critical that the data be used—the data were essentially the justification for undertaking the evaluation in the first place. Failure to use the data may mean that the entire evaluation was a waste.

There are many reasons for collecting the data and using them after collection. These can become action items for the team to ensure that changes and adjustments are made. In addition, the client or sponsor must act to ensure that the uses of data are appropriately addressed.

EXHIBIT 7-4. Use of Evaluation Data

Use of Evaluation Data	Appropriate Level of Data				
	1	2	3	4	5
Adjust program design	✔	✔			
Improve implementation			✔	✔	
Influence application and program impact			✔	✔	
Improve management support for the program			✔	✔	
Improve stakeholder satisfaction			✔	✔	✔
Recognize and reward participants		✔	✔	✔	
Justify or enhance budget				✔	✔
Reduce costs		✔	✔	✔	✔
Market programs in the future	✔		✔	✔	✔

MONITORING PROGRESS

A final element of the implementation process is monitoring the overall progress made and communicating that progress. Although often overlooked, an effective communication plan can help keep the implementation on target and let others know what the ROI Methodology is accomplishing. The elements of a communication plan were discussed in chapter 6.

The initial schedule for implementation of ROI is based on key events or milestones. Routine progress reports should be developed to communicate the status of these events or milestones. Reports are usually developed at six-month intervals, but may be more frequent for short-term projects. Two target audiences, the employee engagement team and senior managers, are critical for progress reporting. All team members should be kept informed of the progress, and senior managers should know the extent to which ROI is being implemented and how it is working within the organization.

FINAL THOUGHTS

Even the best model or process will die if it is not used and sustained. This chapter explored the implementation of the ROI process. If not approached in a systematic, logical, and planned way, the ROI process will not be an integral part of the employee engagement evaluation efforts, and accountability will suffer. This chapter presented the different elements that must be considered and issues that must be addressed to ensure that implementation is smooth and uneventful. Smooth implementation is the most effective means of overcoming resistance to ROI. The result provides a complete integration of ROI as a mainstream component of major projects.

The first part of this book outlined the relevant steps necessary to use the ROI Methodology with employee engagement programs. In the next part we share case studies illustrating how the ROI process was applied to different employee engagement programs.

Part II
Evaluation in Action
Case Studies on the Evaluation of
Employee Engagement

8

Measuring ROI in Employee Engagement With a Bonus

National Crushed Stone Company

Jack J. Phillips and Patti P. Phillips

This case was prepared to serve as a basis for discussion rather than to illustrate either effective or ineffective administrative and management practices. All names, dates, places, and organizations have been disguised at the request of the author or organization.

Abstract

Set in an extremely competitive industry, this case study shows the impact and return on investment of an employee engagement system with a significant bonus attached. Because of a lack of engagement, National Crushed Stone, a large construction aggregates company, decided to pilot a program of revised employee engagement coupled with gainsharing. The company was able to develop indisputable data to show the contribution of the new program and the effects that it had on operations.

BACKGROUND

The crushed stone industry is a very competitive industry where profit margins are narrow and cost control is everything. Companies in this industry are constantly seeking ways to control costs to gain a competitive advantage in the marketplace. National Crushed Stone (NCS) is one of the leading firms in the crushed stone industry, with more than 300 locations in several geographic areas. Each crushed stone plant offers a narrowly defined product mix, consisting of various sizes of crushed stone that is used in construction projects such as roads, bridges, and large buildings. NCS takes pride in its employee relations programs and usually has a stable workforce, although turnover can be a problem. A typical plant is staffed with approximately 20 employees and is managed by a plant manager. Employees perform a variety of jobs from entry-level labor duties to skilled mechanic positions involving equipment repair. They are assigned to one of 12 different job titles within a plant. Each job has a distinctive pay rate, and employees usually work in their specific job classifications all day.

THE ENGAGEMENT ISSUE

A crushed stone plant must constantly control costs to be a survivor in the industry. Crushed stone is a very common commodity, but the price is low on the per ton basis, averaging about six dollars a ton. Rock quarries are located near market areas where the stone is needed to build roads, bridges, and shopping centers, because hauling the stone creates cost. For example, if the rock quarry is 50 miles away, there will be as much in the cost of the transportation as there is in the product itself. Thus, a quarry operator must operate on low cost to make a profit.

There are some concerns that the costs at NCS were not as low as they could be, although they were among the lowest in the industry. Some costs are fixed and not under the control of the quarry team. For example, the local plant cannot control royalties or property lease costs. However, many costs can be controlled. The suggestion is that if employees are really engaged in quarry operations, taking a very strong interest in maintaining the equipment, taking care of the equipment, working smarter, and operating in an efficient way, the costs could be lower, perhaps even significantly so.

The operations vice president is really proud of his ability to maintain very efficient plants and was skeptical when the HR executive approached him about getting employees more involved in taking care of the work, the equipment, and the quarry. But he was willing to listen. The HR team suggested a simple employee engagement survey, the results of which are shown in Exhibit 8-1.

The scores were very low on the six critical statements (questions 1, 2, 5, 8, 9, and 10). To a certain extent, this confirmed that there was a lack of engagement. The HR executive proposed that if employees become more engaged, at least in most of the statements, they will take more interest in their jobs, try to be more efficient, take care of equipment, take care of the plant, and even make suggestions for improving.

However, the company culture wasn't very open to employees accepting responsibility, making recommendations, and being involved in making decisions. In this business, a typical rock quarry had a capable superintendent who gave the orders, made the decisions, and expected people to work, obeying orders and following directions. In order to implement this plan, NCS would have to change its culture. It also made the decision to retitle the superintendents as plant managers, and give them the additional expectation of having a more involved and engaged workforce. But this does not happen just by decree, discussion, meeting, memo, or policy—it comes from changing the mindset of the organization while adjusting job descriptions and encouraging employees to open up.

Exhibit 8-1. Engagement Survey Issues

Topic	Scores
1. My suggestions to improve work are welcomed.	2.15
2. I accept responsibility for my work.	2.19
3. I have great co-workers at work.	3.91
4. My work expectations are clear.	3.22
5. I routinely receive recognition for my good work.	2.15
6. My performance is often discussed.	2.61
7. I have opportunities to learn at work.	3.78
8. I am encouraged to do my best.	2.32
9. I am involved in decisions at work.	2.05
10. I have everything I need to do a good job.	2.77

5-point scale: 1 = Not at all, 5 = Very much

The plant managers viewed this approach with some skepticism because they were not sure that the move would make a difference, at least not enough to overcome the cost of the program. Many of them came from the old-line management where the boss was the boss and everyone else took the orders. NCS was trying to change that mentality by bringing in more open-minded managers who had college degrees and believed in participatory management and having employees involved in the process.

In early discussions, it was suggested that a portion of the cost savings be shared with the employees. There is no better way to recognize the efforts of employees than to reward them with a bonus that is tied to their performance. Using a concept called gainsharing, the decision was made to share half the gains in cost reductions with employees, providing a bonus for becoming more engaged, taking actions, and exploring options for lower costs. This concept has been successful in several areas, but until this study, there was no indication that it had been used with rock quarries.

The attractiveness of the concept was met with some resistance. Philosophically, plant managers had difficulty with the concepts of:
* sharing sensitive cost data with employees
* having employees more involved in the decisions
* allowing employees to make suggestions for improving operations.

Fortunately, they were open to trying the process to see if it worked; if successful, the bonus could be significant.

ROI DRIVERS

The HR executive knew that others were concerned about the value of the project. Investments of time would be substantial and senior management wanted some indication of the payoff before pursuing full implementation. The payoff would have to go beyond the traditional positive feedback from employees and an occasional report showing reduced costs. It needed a comprehensive evaluation, up to and including measuring the return on investment. This way, the HR executive reasoned, senior managers could see the new system as a value-added process that would help the company reach its major goals of increased efficiency and greater profits.

This is an excellent example of a program beginning with the end in mind: business impact measures. The HR executive anticipated that the program would reduce labor cost per ton and employee turnover. In addition, as employees became more engaged, absenteeism was expected to decline, and job satisfaction to improve. While these benefits had been attributed to engagement in other settings, proof was necessary to convince plant managers to fully embrace the concept. Armed with the determination to show the value of the program, the HR executive, with the support of the VP of operations, pursued the development and implementation of the program on a pilot basis.

Development and Implementation

The new system was planned for implementation in six locations that represented typical NCS plants. The complete process, which would comprise several stages, was developed during a two-month period using the part-time assistance of an external consultant and two internal staff members.

The first phase was to review the cost statements with the plan to present them to the employees. It was decided that only the controllable costs would be included and they would be in a format that would make it easy for the average employee to see and appreciate. They identified the particular cost items where employees could make a difference if they were more engaged in the process. Some of these controllable costs included equipment maintenance costs, conveyer belt expenses, plant maintenance, tire costs, fuel costs, quality, water, electricity, labor, and accidents.

Phase two involved developing potential actions that employees could take to improve each of these measures. These actions would come out of discussions with employees. The plan was to have meetings with employees, tackle a particular cost item at each meeting, and focus on how to improve it. Although more input and action would be requested from the entire group, they would start with potential actions that could be taken for each category.

Phase three focused on amending the job responsibilities to ensure that they were written in a manner that would cause employees to assume more responsibility, expanding job duties beyond the classic "what you do" and including how to measure work, what they can change, and how they can control the work. Employees would have the responsibility to speak up, take actions, and help make decisions.

Phase four involved structuring the plant meetings, which would be conducted by the plant manager and a representative from HR. In addition, the VP of operations and operations managers would be invited to attend if feasible. The meetings would be for reviewing the cost data, comparing it with the budget, and then highlighting critical areas where focus is needed. Then, they could deep dive into one cost item more specifically. As the meetings progressed during the year, they started with the cost item with the most opportunity and worked down the list. By the end of the year, the least cost item would be discussed.

Phase five involved the design of the gainsharing process. The design essentially follows these rules:

- The cost for each category is set for the budget for the year based on what the plant managers and the area operations manager believes to be possible. This is the typical approach each year. The budget becomes the target for employees.
- As employees come under the budget, they receive half the savings, to be paid quarterly.
- Following this process, there will be a larger bonus in the last quarter compared with first quarter.
- For the next year, the new target is the previous budget plus a small amount for inflation, using the producer price index as the measurement for adjusting the budget.

Although, after the first year, there is a lower number for each cost item, the team did not expect that number to continue to be reduced. The cost savings opportunities just won't be there. If the target is reset with a lower number, it would demotivate the employees and they would give up. The new target should be the original target adjusted for what would have probably been the new budget considering inflation. This is a great motivator because as employees achieve a lower cost they are rewarded for continuing to reduce costs. Because the company is willing to share half of that to keep the lower costs, it is a win-win situation for all parties.

Phase six was the plant managers' workshop for the six plant managers involved in this pilot group. This one-day workshop taught them the concepts of engagement, their roles in the process, how their jobs are shifting, how the process works, and the gainsharing rewards for everyone. Incidentally, the plant managers were already paid a bonus depending on meeting certain goals. If they have a lower cost than budgeted, then they would receive a much better bonus.

Phase seven involved an introductory two-hour training session with employees to introduce the process, show how it works, and explain their particular role in the process.

EVALUATION METHODOLOGY

To ensure that the new system received a comprehensive evaluation, the five-level framework for evaluation was undertaken and the actual calculation of the return on investment was planned using the ROI Methodology. Data would be collected to obtain the reaction from employees (Level 1) and to measure the extent to which they learned the new approach and how the gainsharing process works (Level 2). In addition, employees' progress would be monitored on the job to determine how engaged they are at each plant (Level 3). Also, specific cost measures and other impacts (Level 4) would be monitored at each plant before and after the program, and these data would be compared with a group of similar plants. This control group arrangement involved identifying six other crushed stone plants to compare with the six plants destined for implementation. This approach should ensure that the results achieved were directly related to the new system. The actual cost of the system would be compared with the monetary value of the benefits to develop an actual ROI (Level 5). To be conservative, one year of monetary benefits would be obtained and compared with the fully loaded costs. The new system was expected to represent a positive return in the seventh year, so a one-year payoff is underestimating the results.

Process Model

These five levels represent a logical flow of data. The ROI Methodology uses a logic model to ensure that the project delivers value. The beginning point for a project is to set objectives. Under this methodology, objectives are set for five levels: reaction, learning, application, impact, and ROI. This provides the proper focus throughout the project, as individuals react properly, learn what to do, make it successful, and then have the desired impact.

Exhibit 8-2 shows the 10-step ROI process model that illustrates the logical flow of data, moving through the different phases of each step, up to and including reporting the results to various stakeholders. Critical parts of this model are to collect the proper data from the different levels, isolate the effects of the project from other influences, ensure that conservative methods are used to convert data to money, and set the value stream for the benefits. Many projects pay off in one year; others will be multiple years. This decision is made at the beginning of the project. Another important issue is to ensure that the intangibles are captured and properly connected to the project. Then, the results must be communicated to a variety of stakeholders, with the key client being the principal audience.

EXHIBIT 8-2. ROI Methodology

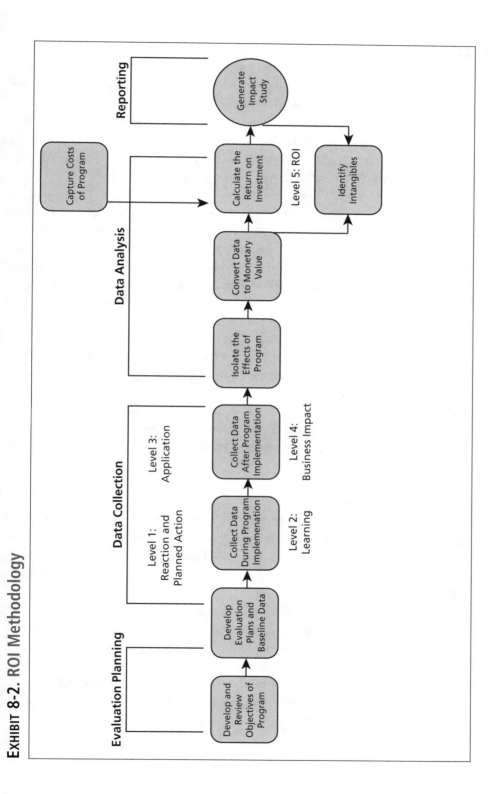

Standards

Any process model needs standards. The 12 guiding principles for the ROI Methodology are:

1. When conducting a higher-level evaluation, collect data at lower levels.
2. When planning a higher-level evaluation, the previous level of evaluation is not required to be comprehensive.
3. When collecting and analyzing data, use only the most credible sources.
4. When analyzing data, select the most conservative alternatives for calculations.
5. Use at least one method to isolate the effects of the program or project.
6. If no improvement data are available for a population or from a specific source, assume that no improvement has occurred.
7. Adjust estimates of improvements for the potential error of the estimates.
8. Avoid use of extreme data items and unsupported claims when calculating ROI calculations.
9. Use only the first year of annual benefits in the ROI analysis of short-term solutions.
10. Fully load all costs of the solution, project, or program when analyzing ROI.
11. Intangible measures are defined as measures that are purposely not converted to monetary values.
12. Communicate the results of the ROI Methodology to all key stakeholders.

The standards are very conservative, which is particularly CEO- and CFO-friendly. They provide the guidance so that projects are consistent, but conservative in their analysis.

Control Group Selection

Selecting specific plants to use in a control group represented a challenging issue. Although as many as 30 variables can influence the performance of a crushed stone plant, only a small group of variables could be used, on a practical basis, to select the two groups. The area operations managers of the six selected locations identified the top five variables as:

- the size of the plant, in terms of annual production
- the product mix of the plant; some products require more time to produce and are more abrasive to the equipment
- the market, as defined by the construction activity in the local market area
- the age of the equipment, which is already a routinely monitored variable; older equipment can cause inefficiencies in production
- previous plant productivity.

In addition, three more variables were considered: the average wage rate, unplanned absenteeism, and the employee turnover rate. These additional variables should be similar because they were closely related to the perceived payoff of the program.

These eight variables were used to select six locations to compare with the six locations where the plan would be implemented. Exhibit 8-3 shows the average wage, absenteeism, turnover rate, employee level, and production prior to program implementation for both the pilot group and the control group.

EXHIBIT 8-3. Wage and Turnover Data for Both Groups—One-Year Average Before Implementation

	Employment Level	Average Wage	Unplanned Absenteeism	Voluntary Turnover	Production (millions of tons)
Plants With New System	126	$20.15	7.4%	18%	8.5
Plants Without New System	132	$20.31	7.8%	19%	8.9

SYSTEM DESIGN

Before the engagement system could be fully implemented, job descriptions and responsibilities had to be broadened to indicate more responsibility and accountability. The descriptions were written in a tone that encourages the employees to do more, seek more, and become more. With these descriptions in place, the engagement was then defined.

The engagement survey that was administered as part of the needs assessment was the beginning point to determine what types of issues should be addressed. After much input from the plant managers, senior executives, and employees, coupled with a review of the literature on engagement, a new definition of engagement was developed as shown in Exhibit 8-4. This breaks down the process to achieve results with engagement by first detailing the six items employees need from their jobs. Next, the five items of what employees must actually see and experience in the work setting are identified. More importantly, it identifies the seven items that employees must do as they take a more active role and make some improvements leading to the desired impact. This initial list was a starting point that showed where adjustments needed to be made.

A workshop was conducted with plant managers to teach them how to engage employees, using these concepts and the ratings of the employee-only concepts. The managers learned how to make these adjustments, make changes, and support the process in a productive way.

Exhibit 8-4. Engagement Defined

What Employees *Need*	What Employees Must *See*	What Employees Must *Do*
• Opportunity to grow • Increase in pay in proportion to contribution • Recognition for the good work they do • To be appreciated for their work • An opportunity to do their best work • Clear expectations	• Routine feedback from managers • A future in the organization • Learning opportunities on the job • A supportive environment • Work that is important	• Take responsibility for results • Use unique talent to make a contribution • Take a more active role in decisions • Offer suggestions for improvement • Collaborate more with co-workers • Control the work and make adjustments • Perform high-quality work

Next, monthly meetings were organized. The first meeting, which was a two-hour workshop, focused on the description of the program, the details of the complete system, and the employees' role in the process. Following that, monthly meetings were held to work on cost items. This cycle would be repeated each year, with a continued focus on the major cost items, with the most important cost tackled first and the less important costs left for later.

Finally, the gainsharing system was developed to share gains with the employees, who would receive half the difference between the budget costs and actual costs. This amount would be paid quarterly during the meetings. The complete system design formed a process that will be constantly revised and adjusted as the program is implemented and sustained.

EVALUATION PLANNING

Planning the evaluation is a key step in measuring the effectiveness of a successful implementation. Detailed planning includes determining the methods for data collection, isolating the effects of the new system, converting data to monetary values, and deciding which costs to capture. The two planning documents used in this analysis are presented as Exhibits 8-5 and 8-6. Exhibit 8-5 shows the data collection plan, which includes collecting data for Level 1 (reaction to the system), Level 2 (learning how the system works), Level 3 (application of the system), and Level 4 (business impact). It also shows the specific data collection methods and the timing for data collection, as well as defining the responsibilities. Exhibit 8-6 presents the plan for the ROI analysis, which includes detailing how the effects of the system will be isolated from other influences and how the data will be converted to monetary values. In addition, the specific cost categories of the program are detailed, along with other important issues concerning the overall evaluation plan.

Exhibit 8-5. Data Collection Plan

Program: _____   Responsibility: _____

Level	Program Objective(s)	Data Collection Methods or Instruments	Timing of Data Collection	Responsibilities for Data Collection
1	**REACTION AND PLANNED ACTION** • Relevance of new system to the work • Importance of new system to NCS • Importance of new system to my success • Motivational effect of new system • Intent to use new system	• Questionnaire (2 pages)	• End of initial meeting about new system	• HR representative
2	**LEARNING** • Engagement concepts • Job responsibilities change • Brainstorming process • Gainsharing fundamentals • How the system works	• Objective test: true-false and multiple choice (15 items) • 70 percent success	• End of initial meeting about new system	• HR representative
3	**APPLICATION AND IMPLEMENTATION** • Increased engagement • Increased participants • More responsibilities	• Survey to employees • Questionnaire to plant managers and employees	• 3 months after implementation	• HR representative • External consultant
4	**BUSINESS IMPACT** • Reduce variable costs per ton • Reduce employee turnover • Reduce absenteeism	• Monitor records	• 6 months and 1 year after implementation	• HR representative • External consultant
5	ROI	Comments: Need to get stakeholder input.		

Exhibit 8-6. ROI Analysis Plan

Program: _____   Responsibility: _____   Date: _____

Data Items	Methods for Isolating the Effects of the Program	Methods of Converting Data to Monetary Values	Cost Categories	Intangible Benefits	Other Influences/ Issues	Communication Targets
Cost per ton	Control group arrangement	Direct conversion-cost savings	• Needs assessment • Development • Administration • Plant manager time • Employee time • Training and meetings • Materials • Travel and lodging • Plant manager workshop • Bonus pay • Evaluation	• Job satisfaction • Teamwork • Customer satisfaction • Customer complaints • Quality • Downtime	• Avoid peak season, if possible • No communication with control group • Watch for Hawthorne effect	• Employees • Plant managers • Area operation managers • Production manager • Senior executives • Other plant managers • HR staff
Employee turnover	Control group arrangement	Industry data from study-adjusted for company				
Absenteeism	Control group arrangement	Estimate from the HR team				

RESULTS: REACTION AND LEARNING

It was considered important for employees to learn about the new system and react favorably to it. Although a positive reaction was assumed, employee feedback was obtained in a more formal method using a one-page questionnaire. This was considered necessary because of potential skepticism from management and the sensitivity of making adjustments to the job and adding a bonus. The questionnaire was designed to capture specific reaction in five areas, as shown in Exhibit 8-7, which also includes reactions from the plant manager on the same set of measures. Both employees and plant managers provided reactions that exceeded the expectations. This is critical to have success later.

EXHIBIT 8-7. Reaction Results

Topic	Rating (Manager)	Rating (Employees)
1. Relevance of the engagement system to the work of employees.	4.00	4.06
2. The importance of this system to NCS.	4.20	4.22
3. The importance of this system to employee success.	4.40	4.61
4. The motivational effect of the system.	4.40	4.74
5. The intent to use the system properly.	4.20	4.35

5-point scale: 1 = Not at all, 5 = Very much

For Level 2 (learning), a simple true/false and multiple-choice test was administered, using three questions about each part, for a total of 15. Exhibit 8-8 shows the results for this level from employees, which exceeded the goal of 70 percent minimum score.

EXHIBIT 8-8. Learning Results

Topic	Score
The engagement concepts	2.2
Job description and responsibilities changes	2.1
Brainstorming process	1.8
Gainsharing fundamentals	2.6
How the system works	2.5
Total	11.2

5-point scale: 1 = Not at all, 5 = Very much

APPLICATION AND USE

The important part of the study is to understand clearly if the employees are more engaged. A revised engagement instrument, based on the issues in Exhibit 8-4, was administered just before the program was launched with the six pilot plants. Then a post-survey was administered three months later. The results are presented in Exhibit 8-9.

Exhibit 8-9. Engagement Survey Results

Engagement Issue	Pre-Survey	Post-Survey
What Employees *Need* (six questions)	3.19	4.09
What Employees Must *See* (five questions)	2.92	4.27
What Employees Must *Do* (seven questions)	3.05	4.52

5-point scale: 1 = Not at all, 5 = Very much

Overall the improvements were significant and impressive. It is also important to capture data about how employees are participating in meetings, taking a more responsible role, accepting accountability for results, and sharing information freely with others. Data were collected from the employees and their plant managers. Data from the managers were based on observation, whereas the data from the employees were collected using a questionnaire to determine their perception of what they were actually doing. Exhibit 8-10 shows the Level 3 application data taken from both employees and the plant manager.

Exhibit 8-10. Engagement Implementation

System Issue	Rating (Employee)	Rating (Manager)
1. Using engagement concepts	4.12	4.20
2. Participating in meetings	4.22	3.40
3. Taking a more responsible role	4.70	3.60
4. Accepting accountability for results	4.78	3.60
5. Sharing information freely	4.47	4.20
6. Using the system properly	4.17	4.20

5-point scale: 1 = Not at all, 5 = Very much

BUSINESS IMPACT

It is important to clearly understand the impact of the program. Impact data are derived directly from the system. The cost per ton for each cost category was monitored, along with turnover and absenteeism. Exhibit 8-11 shows the cost per ton for before and after the program. It also shows the turnover rate, which is reported monthly but annualized, and the absenteeism rate, which is the percent of individuals absent on any given day. This is restricted to the unplanned absenteeism category.

The data showed a dramatic improvement in impact caused by the program, with the exception in total employment and production, which remained similar between the control and pilot plants. The cost per ton for the variable costs showed a dramatic improvement for the experimental plants, with a reduction of 31 cents per ton. However, because there was also a five cent per ton reduction in the plants without the system, this five cent per ton must be subtracted from the 31 cents to yield 26 cent improvement.

The same approach was taken for volunteer turnover. The experimental plants saw a significant reduction from 18 percent down to 12 percent. Because the control plants also saw a 1 percent reduction, that 1 percent is subtracted. Thus the program saw a 5 percent improvement.

Unplanned absenteeism saw a dramatic reduction from 7.4 percent to 4.2 percent for the experimental plants. There was a slight reduction (0.1 percent) in the control plant, which was also subtracted to give the overall improvement. This shows a very dramatic improvement and the method of isolation used is the best method.

From all indications, nothing unusual was happening in the six plants that could have affected results (such as a sudden market shift, weather issues, a change in plant manager, or other factors). So, it appears that these plants were matched up very well and were consistent throughout the year-long study period.

Exhibit 8-11. Business Impact Results

	Total Employees		Annual Production (Millions)		Variable Cost per Ton		Voluntary Turnover		Unplanned Absenteeism	
	Before	After	Before	After	Before	After	Before	After	Before	After
Plants With New System	126	125	8.5	8.6	$3.19	$2.88	18%	12%	7.4%	4.2%
Plants Without New System	132	130	8.9	8.9	$3.22	$3.17	19%	18%	7.8%	7.7%

CONVERTING DATA TO MONEY

Converting the data to money was relatively easy in this case because the measures are already in the organization.

Monetary Values

For the variable production, costs are expressed in money as cents per ton, so no conversion was necessary. This is the principal measure connected with the project. The data suggested that for this mix of employees (production workers and some skilled workers), the voluntary turnover cost would be about 50 percent of annual pay, and management agreed to this value before the system was implemented. These studies were based on having a fully loaded cost for turnover, to include recruiting, selection, and onboarding, as well as training and improvement, until the employees were up to previous levels. It also includes disruption caused by the departing employees and the premium pay necessary for other employees to do the job, as well as supervisor time and exit costs. Thus this cost figure seems very conservative.

Finally, the absenteeism cost was straightforward and the group agreed the estimated cost would be calculated at $160. This is probably lower than the actual number, but the key is that it was agreed on in advance.

There were also a few intangibles that could have been converted to money. For example, the slight reduction in the number of loads of stone that were rejected by the customer could have been attributed to the program. However, the number was small and it would require some extra work to calculate the actual money savings, because the quality team had not calculated the average cost previously. In addition, another intangible cost that could have been attributed to the program was a decrease in the amount of downtime for the entire plant. Most of the team thought that it was because of this program, as the employees took good care of the plant and provided better plant maintenance. However, the number was small and there was no credible monetary value for one hour of downtime. Consequently, both of these were left as intangible, as described in a later section.

Monetary Benefits of Project

Exhibit 8-12 shows the calculation of the monetary benefits. The 26 cent cost per ton improvement in total production (8,600,000 tons) gave a bonus pool of $2,236,000 to be spilt equally with employees and the company. This yielded a bonus of $9,395 annually for the employees, which was about a 22 percent bonus over their base pay. This, indeed, is a powerful motivator. In addition, it represents a huge amount of savings directly to the company's bottom line as the monetary benefit for this program: a total of $1,118,000.

EXHIBIT 8-12. Monetary Benefits

Production Costs
31¢ - 5¢ = 26¢ per ton
8,600,000 tons × 26¢ = $2,236,000 bonus pool
$$\text{Split} = \frac{\$2,236,000}{2} = \$1,118,000$$

Payout to Employees
125 - 6 = 119 eligible employees
$$\frac{\$1,118,000}{119} = \$9,395 \text{ per employee}$$
Benefit to employee = 22 percent bonus
Benefit to company = $1,118,000

Turnover Costs
18% - 12% = 6% - 1% = 5%
119 × 5% = 6 turnovers prevented
Annual salary = $20.15 × 2080 = $41,912
Cost per turnover = 50% of annual salary = $20,956
Benefits = $20,956 × 6 = $125,736

Absenteeism Costs
7.4% - 4.2% = 3.2% - 0.1% = 3.1%
Total possible days: 240 days × 119 = 28,560 days
Prevented: 28,560 × 3.1% = 885 days
Cost per day = $160
Benefits = 885 × 160 = $141,600
Total benefits = $1,118,000 + $125,736 + $141,600 = $1,385,336

Turnover costs were calculated very similarly, with this program preventing 5 percent turnover, which would annualize to yield six turnovers prevented for the company. Plugging in the value of the cost of a turnover, there was an improvement of $125,736.

Absenteeism costs were very straightforward, with a 3.1 percent reduction as a result of this program. When this is multiplied by the total number of days that employees could work, this 3.1 percent absenteeism reduction accounts for 885 days prevented. When this value is multiplied by the cost of an absence, the result is $141,600. In summary, there is a total benefit of $1,385,336 for one year of this program.

PROGRAM COSTS AND ROI

Costs

Exhibit 8-13 shows the total cost for the program by various categories. The needs assessment cost is estimated to be $18,000, which includes the cost of the initial analysis, the first engagement survey with a sample of employees, some various meetings, literature searches, and an external consultant. When this is prorated over 6,000 employees, who would be eligible for the program—and calculated systemwide for all 300 facilities, this yields $3 per employee. When multiplied by the 121 employees who were involved at the beginning of the study, the yield is $363, which is not significant because of the large number of employees who would be eligible. Proration is the right thing to do because if the program is implemented systemwide, this cost would be prorated over the entire process.

The same approach is taken for the system development cost of $30,000, which includes adjusting the job descriptions and duties, developing the gainsharing plan, and developing an entire series of meetings for the program. Content development was also accounted for through developing the workshops for the plant managers and the initial two-hour workshop for the employees. The engagement design was a redesign of the engagement survey from the original document, formatted to fit what the organization was attempting to do; it was tested and administered at two different times. The initial development cost was $10,000, but the actual survey administration including time and travel of the team was $12,440.

Program materials costs were small. Travel and lodging for the managers and HR staff who attended the monthly meetings at all six plants for a year made up a significant portion of the cost. The workshop facilitation and coordination for time and travel was also included. The facilities and refreshments were minimal (about $100 per meeting). Some meetings were held over breakfast, some were at lunch, and some were just during a coffee break. Another expense was the participants' time for the meetings, including the two-hour workshop. Some would argue that this cost was already in the system (all plant-related costs should be in the system on a cost per ton basis for the variable costs). However, to be extremely credible and conservative, these costs were calculated for all the employees who were taken off production for the two-hour workshop and approximately one hour for each meeting. Finally, the plant managers' time was included, along with a very small overhead allocation. Costs for the ROI evaluation study, which was conducted by the staff, also included the time and travel required to present the results to different groups. This totaled $129,886.

ROI Calculation

The benefit-cost ratio and ROI were calculated and are shown. For every dollar invested, there was $10.70 in benefits, which is extremely high by any BCR calculation. In addition, the ROI was calculated to be 967 percent, which means that for every dollar invested in this program, another $9.67 was returned after the dollar is recovered. This is really significant.

$$ BCR = \frac{\$1,385,336}{\$129,886} = 10.67 $$

$$ ROI = \frac{\$1,385,336 - \$129,886}{\$129,886} \times 100 = 967\% $$

INTANGIBLE BENEFITS

Although measurable and convertible to monetary values in some cases, the intangibles were considered significant but were not used in the ROI analysis. Several intangible benefits were identified and connected to the project, including job satisfaction, teamwork, customer satisfaction, the number of customer complaints, the number of loads of stone rejected by the customer, and the amount of plant downtime. The last two, quality of the stone and plant downtime, could possibly have been converted to money, but were not because of the extra time involved.

CONCLUSIONS

The results are very impressive, exceeding the expectations of all involved. The VP of operations was amazed at the reduction in cost and did not think that it was possible to make that much of a difference. Armed with this initial first year of results, he made the recommendation to set the next budget at the previous level, adjusted for the producer price index. This will be the budget going forward. If the team maintains this same level of performance, their bonus will increase as the producer price index increases. If the team can further reduce costs, the bonus will be even greater. The value of this program is almost a no brainer. However, there was a fear that the project might not work for the long term, and ultimately could cause some problems. These concerns will be faced when that point comes.

Exhibit 8-13. Program Cost Summary

Needs assessment (prorated over all eligible employees) $18,000 ÷ 6,000 employees = 3 × 121	$363
System development including adjusting job description (prorated over all eligible employees) $30,000 ÷ 6,000 = 5 × 121	$605
Content development for workshops (prorated over all eligible employees) $12,000 ÷ 6,000 = 2 × 121	$242
Engagement design (prorated over all eligible employees) $10,000 ÷ 6,000 = 1.67 × 121	$202
Engagement surveys: time and travel $12,440	$12,440
Program materials $20 × 121	$2,420
Meetings travel and lodging: manager and HR staff $29,440	$29,440
Workshop facilitation and coordination: time and travel $2,000 × 7 days of facilitation, travel, and coordination	$14,000
Facilities and refreshments 72 days at $100 cost per day	$7,200
Participants time: salaries plus benefits (30 percent benefits factor) 14 hrs × 121 × $20.15 × 1.3	$44,374
Salaries plus benefits 20 hrs × 6 managers × $47.00/hr	$5,640
Overhead	$2,000
ROI evaluation	$11,000
Total	**$129,886**

Credibility of Data

It is important for the study to have credible results. When employee engagement is connected to plant cost in this type of program, there are always questions about the credibility of the results. This program has an even stronger need for credibility due to the bonus associated with increased employee engagement. The results of this study are credible for several reasons:

- The three business impact data are records that came out of the system and were reported routinely to each plant.
- The method used to separate the effect of the experimental group from the control group represents the best research approach.
- All the costs were included, even the indirect costs that are often debatable. This is an attempt to make sure that no expense item was left out of the study.
- The payoff for this program is based on one year. This program would have multiple-year payoffs and perhaps a little less cost going forward because the meetings can be integrated into the work of the plant manager or area manager.
- A balanced profile of the financial and nonfinancial data was presented. There is clear evidence that reactions were favorable, employees learned how to make it work, and they followed through by being more engaged throughout the process.

Recommendation

The data show that this program should be expanded to at least several hundred plants in the near term. The company decided to work with nonunion plants first, to make sure that the program was consistent and worked properly. The unionized plants will require negotiations with the union or union involvement, which will come later.

QUESTIONS FOR DISCUSSION

1. Critique the data collection plan.
2. Critique the approach to isolate the effects of the program.
3. Critique the monetary benefits calculation.
4. Is this credible?
5. Are there any recommendations you would make?
6. Is the ROI realistic?
7. How should the ROI be communicated to senior management?
8. Should this system be implemented at other locations?
9. Sometimes a preprogram forecast is needed before attempting to implement the new system. Is this possible for this scenario? If so, how?

9

Measuring ROI in Employee Engagement With a Broad Focus

Home Furnishing Stores

Jack J. Phillips and Patti P. Phillips

This case was prepared to serve as a basis for discussion rather than to illustrate either effective or ineffective administrative and management practices. All names, dates, places, and organizations have been disguised at the request of the author or organization.

Abstract

This large chain of home furnishing stores with popular brands is pushing for more growth, increased profitability, and more talent performance. Although the chain is very successful, top executives and the HR team believed that better performance was possible, particularly if employees were more engaged. The concept of engagement was pushed beyond just being engaged with work but also being engaged with customers and the community. With this broader definition of engagement, the chain implemented a comprehensive revised employee engagement program with impressive results. The combination of making adjustments in responsibilities, changing the definition of engagement, and utilizing the creativity, experience, and smart thinking of employees was what made this program successful. Store managers were involved, a new engagement survey instrument was developed, e-learning was used to focus on seven components of engagement, workshops were conducted for both the employees and managers, and online support helped to deliver a very positive ROI to the executives.

BACKGROUND

Home Furnishing Stores (HFS) is a large international retailer for several major brands. Some brands exist within their major store name and locations; other brands represent stand-alone stores for the brand and integrate with the overall products. HFS operates in more than 20 countries with more than 40,000 employees. Customers can purchase items in the store, have items delivered to their home, or have items delivered to a pickup center. As with many other retailers, HFS is shifting to an e-commerce option and the executives want to make sure the same excellent customer experience that is offered in-store is also felt online.

HFS, which is traded on the New York Stock Exchange, has been a good investment for shareholders. However, in a very competitive industry, and with the ups and downs of global markets, HFS wants to place additional focus on making the stores more profitable and growing both the number of stores and the e-commerce platform. While there are many facets that drive store profitability and growth, most of it rests with the talent in the organization. Their focus is on the employees who work directly with the customers and procure their products (procurement) and who distribute the products to the various customers and locations (distribution centers).

Vision

There is usually some debate on which stakeholder group is more important to the success of the organization. Some would indicate that the investors are more critical because, without them, there is no company. The goal of the company is to provide a good return on investment through share price growth and dividends. Others would say that the customers make the difference. Without the customers, there are no sales and the goal is to attract great customers and keep them for a long time. Still, others would say none of this occurs without great talent in the stores, distribution centers, and procurement function. Together they make it work. The executives at HFS have indicated that while all three groups are important, improvements in the organization have to focus on the employees. The vision for HFS is for it to be truly a great organization. In simple terms, executives want HFS to be a great place to work. This is where employee engagement becomes a critical issue: The company has been a great place to work, but the executives want to make it better. Recent years have seen an excessive rise in employee turnover; executives want to increase engagement to lower turnover and continue to make the company one of the best places to work and attract the best and brightest in the future.

In addition, executives want HFS to be a great place to shop by providing the best customer experience possible, whether customers are in the store or online. They want customers to feel respected, engaged, and nurtured along the way—the same online experience that Zappos has enjoyed and has been reported in several references (Heish 2010). For the in-store sales they want the experience to be extremely pleasant and helpful to make customers return often, purchase more, and stay with them for a long time.

At the same time, with great talent providing a great customer experience, financial performance should follow, increasing the profitability of the stores and allowing investors to receive more return on their investment through dividend and share price growth. From the investment perspective, executives want HFS to be a top performing company. Still, the top executives, and particularly the CEO, wanted to do more. They wanted to make HFS an important part of the community and a great company for the community. This would entail focusing on not only issues such as local health, education, and low-income challenges, but also environmental projects.

Collectively when these four goals are achieved, a very important sustainable enterprise is developed: the vision for the organization.

The Value of Engagement

This new vision places a tremendous focus on employee engagement. The perception is that employee engagement would drive all three subsequent issues: a great place to shop, a great place to invest, and a great company for the community. Exhibit 9-1 shows the connection. By revising the engagement process to focus on broader issues beyond the scope of the work of one individual, the company will be able to achieve several important changes. When employees become engaged with the customer and encourage and support them, the customers become more valuable to the organization. This customer experience will improve customer satisfaction, the net promoter score (NPS), customer loyalty, and customer complaints.

Exhibit 9-1. The Value of Employee Engagement

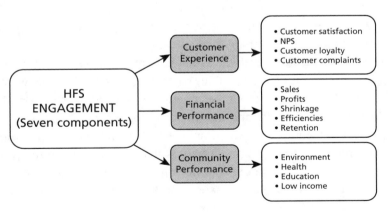

Engagement should connect directly to sales growth, profit improvement, shrinkage reduction, improved efficiencies, and increased retention. These are classic outputs from employee engagement and should be a substantial part of the process to improve the organization's financial performance.

Having employees become more involved and engaged in the community provides much support and assistance where stores are located and distribution centers are placed. Locally, they can help with education issues if employees volunteer for projects in school systems. They can work in low-income areas if the company sponsors projects aimed at uplifting people. And finally, HFS employees could help the environment by participating in recycling programs, efficient fuel consumption, energy conservation, and other important areas.

This perception of employee engagement provides a backdrop for major revisions in an employee engagement program in order to achieve these significant outcomes.

The Analysis

The HR team went about the process of making these changes. The team began with the end in mind, which were the goals shown in Exhibit 9-1, and asked a few questions, including "How can engagement make this improvement?" and "What must employees be doing in the future that they are not doing now that can have such an important impact on customers, financial performance, and the community?" This analysis involved several phases to make sure that an employee engagement program is the proper solution and is clearly connected to the business.

Stage 1: Review literature on engagement. Fortunately, there are many examples of outstanding companies that have been built on the shoulders of fully engaged, committed, and connected employees. These examples covered the three areas of customer experience, financial performance, and community performance.

Stage 2: Review the current status of engagement. Although HFS employees were already engaged and the company was already using standard engagement instruments, there was a feeling that this was not enough. This was because there wasn't a broad enough definition of engagement, some of the existing scores were not where they should be, and some of the issues needed to strengthened beyond just engagement to include accountability and responsibility for success.

Stage 3: Form focus groups with employees. Several focus groups were conducted to see what employees thought might be possible after reviewing the proposed concepts to strengthen engagement. The focus groups met with great excitement and enthusiasm, and suggested some changes and adjustments that would make them better. This created a lot of interest in the program.

Stage 4: Form focus groups with managers. Although the store managers would work together throughout the process, the company held separate focus groups to see how management team would react to the program and to see what was feasible. It also wanted to know what the managers would support and achieve in the demanding environment of retail stores. Again, great input was received, which led to more adjustments to the process to make it better.

Stage 5: Conduct interviews with senior executives. Several interviews were conducted to show the draft of the program and how it linked to the business. With these inputs, the team was ready to design and implement the program.

THE APPROACH

Once employee engagement was redefined with its many facets, the process was ready for execution. The challenge was to introduce the program in a way that was meaningful and timely, and with ample support along the way.

Engagement Defined

Exhibit 9-2 shows the seven components of engagement that fit the new definition desired by the company: my role, my team, my customer, my responsibility, my career, my leadership, and my community.

EXHIBIT 9-2. The Components of Engagement

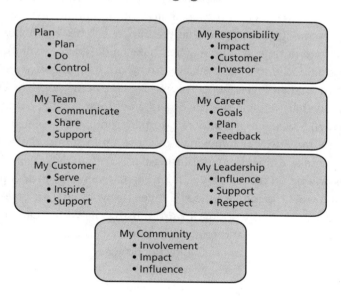

My Role: The beginning point is to redefine the role of work so that all employees can clearly see that they have many responsibilities in their work. They have to plan the work, they have to execute it, and they have to control that work. This involves checking progress, making decisions, and making changes. It is fundamental to engagement to have employees operating in a different way, being more involved in decisions, and checking their progress along the way.

My Team: The company had previously worked in teams in the stores, online, in distribution centers, and in procurement. Although all employees have individual responsibility, it is important for them to help one another and coordinate with the others. This involves continuous communication to share information with one another about the status of individual efforts. An important part of this process is supporting one another, filling in when necessary, and helping out when requested, which all works to make sure that the team functions extremely well as a unit.

My Customer: Here the focus is on working with customers. It is important for employees to provide great customer service in every way possible and inspire customers to have an amazing experience while they are in the store. This will encourage customers to refer others to the store, which will increase the net promoter score. Employees are also encouraged to show customers how to become more engaged. As customers become more involved in learning about products in the store, as well as providing input on new products and suggesting product changes, great things will happen. Customers will become a vast network of decision makers to help provide guidance in the future.

My Responsibility: Along with changes in work, team expectations, and customer expectations comes a change in responsibility and accountability. Here, the focus is not what they are doing as much as what the impact will be. The philosophy must be that the impact and not the activity is what makes a difference, whether it's with the employees closing a sale, the customer returning often, or the investors realizing an improving return on their investment. This requires the outcomes to be clearly focused on improvements that will help the customers, investors, and the community.

My Career: HFS wants to have more internal promotions. To achieve this, career opportunities are provided for individuals to move up in stores, the regions, and the distribution centers and procurement. Career paths had already been developed, but now the focus will be on the employee taking initiatives. This is action is voluntary, suggesting that it will be helpful for the employees to work on their career. This begins with setting clear goals and working toward those goals with a career development plan that is carefully followed and routinely monitored. The key will be the manager's role in providing feedback on progress and supporting employees in their career development efforts.

My Leadership: HFS recognizes that leadership is not just for those who are in leadership positions. Leadership is everywhere. Every person can exhibit leadership by influencing others and by serving as a role model of what should be done or the processes that should be completed. Leadership is also about supporting and serving others, earning respect along the way. Influence, support, and respect are an important part of everyone's leadership dimension.

My Community: To ensure that each HFS location is an important part of the community, employees are encouraged to get involved in an area they would like to pursue. In some cases, some time off may be provided. In others, it's a part-time responsibility. This will be coordinated by the corporate social responsibility team, with individual outcomes monitored along the way. The key is to be involved in some activity that will have an impact in the community that can be connected to their own efforts and influence.

Collectively these seven components provide a much broader definition of engagement, moving from typical engagement with the work itself to other dimensions of the team, the customer, the career, and the community.

Program Design

With a new definition of engagement, the challenge is to introduce the program to the entire team and make it successful in the organization. The program was designed in six steps, as shown in Exhibit 9-3.

EXHIBIT 9-3. Program Design

Preprogram Survey	Engagment Concepts E-Learning	Expectations and Commitment 1-Day Workshop	Leadership Support 1-Day Workshop	Program Support on the Job	Post-Program Survey
Engagement Survey	My role My team My customer My reponsibilities My career My leadership My community	• Program overview • 360% feedback • Review of seven modules • Support available • Coaching • Expectations • Action planning	• Value engagement • How to support program • How to connect • Best practices video • Action planning	• Enagement portal • Engagement survey feedback • Review of seven modules • Support tools • Coaching • Action plan completion	Engagement Survey
All Employees	All Employees	All Employees	Managers Only	All Employees	All Employees

Before a program is rolled out in a new region or area, engagement data are collected using a preprogram survey. Following that, all employees take seven, 30-minute e-learning modules, each of which is aimed at one of the seven components of engagement.

Next, a full-day workshop for associates and managers is conducted. This is designed to provide an overview for the program, and provide feedback on the engagement survey data, which were collected from the employees and managers. It also serves as a quick review of the seven modules, ensuring that everyone has taken the e-learning modules and understands what is involved. Some limited skill practices are conducted, and the support that is available for them to use and reference is described, including the fact that their immediate manager will serve as a coach for the process. Expectations are defined and the concept of action planning is introduced. Action planning involves a particular team, usually led by a manager, and provides the associates and their managers with an opportunity to see how engagement is making a difference with customers, financial performance, and community performance.

The managers attend a second one-day workshop where the value of engagement is clearly outlined, along with tips on how to support the program and make it successful. They also learn how to be an effective coach to their employees. During the workshop they view best-practice videos that show some examples of the behaviors they need to support the seven modules. Some limited skill practices are also conducted with team managers. Finally, each manager selects a team and uses input from their team to choose two measures in the three areas to improve. This begins the action planning process.

The next component is on-the-job training, where the tools, information, and assistance is available to the participants through an engagement portal HFS developed. One-on-one coaching from the manager is available: It may be routinely scheduled or provided on an as-needed basis. Team meetings are often an important part of this program because they allow employees to discuss status, remove obstacles, and suggest enablers. The actions from the action plan are checked off as they are completed, until the desired impact is achieved.

Finally, two months after the program is introduced, a post-program engagement survey is conducted to show the difference between it and the preprogram version. Adjustments are made to the program as needed. Collectively, this design involves the key individuals who are required to make the program work, and it presents everything in a nonthreatening, unbiased way. The program is not focused so much on the performance of individuals, as it is on the performance of the program. Responsibilities and expectations are clearly part of the program and the focus is on having an impact, with engagement being the vehicle to achieve that impact.

EVALUATION APPROACH

HFS's comprehensive engagement program is highly visible, linked to key business objectives, and requires substantial resources. These critical factors, along with the need to identify program successes and improvement opportunities, led to the implementation of an ROI evaluation study using the ROI Methodology. In addition to determining the extent to which the program was increasing engagement capabilities and positively affecting key business measures, the evaluation was positioned to help identify opportunities for improvement for further implementation throughout the organization.

ROI Methodology

A robust evaluation was planned to identify:

- reaction to the program by the associates and managers
- knowledge and skills gained through participation in modules
- success with the application of knowledge and skills in the workplace as associates are more engaged
- barriers and enablers to the application of the knowledge and skills
- business impact and return on investment of the engagement program.

This provided insight into what was working well with the program and opportunities for improvement. Furthermore, evaluation results helped communicate the program's value to increase adoption once it becomes fully integrated into the organization.

The ROI Methodology serves as the structure for designing, planning, and implementing the evaluation study. This approach reports a balanced set of measures, follows a step-by-step process, and adheres to a set of guiding principles that are CEO- and CFO-friendly. These elements ensure a thorough and credible process for communicating the impact of the engagement program to key stakeholders.

The ROI Methodology approach begins with a fundamental framework of categorizing data, which represent measures that capture program success from the participant, system, and economic perspectives. Exhibit 9-4 presents the definition of each level of evaluation data. When combined with intangible data, these five levels tell the complete story of the engagement program's success.

Exhibit 9-4. Evaluation Framework

Level	Measurement Focus
1. Planned Action	Measures participant reaction to the program and planned action
2. Learning	Measures changes in knowledge and skills (engagement concepts)
3. Application and Implementation	Measures changes in actions and on-the-job behavior (engagement)
4. Impact	Measures changes in business impact measures
5. Return on Investment (ROI)	Compares the monetary benefits from the program to the costs of the program

Because the engagement program was comprehensive with many activities, the evaluation required careful planning. Detailed data collection and ROI analysis plans were developed and are presented as Exhibits 9-5 and 9-6.

Data Collection

Exhibit 9-5 shows the data collection plan for this program, which starts with the objectives and defines the measures, data collection method, source, timing, and responsibilities. This is a classic plan for ROI analysis.

ROI Analysis Plan

Exhibit 9-6 presents the ROI analysis plan for this program, and represents a very common approach to this type of analysis. It begins with the business impact measures that are influenced by the program, with each participant selecting at least two measures to improve using the engagement competencies and skills. The method of isolation is the participant's estimate of the program's influence on the impact data. While creating a comparison group would be the best way to show the impact of the program, the experimental versus control group comparison was not feasible because when participants select different measures, matching groups would be almost impossible. With participant estimates, the data are collected in a nonthreatening, nonbiased way, and there are adjustments for error in their estimates. Standard items (presented later) provided to participants in the workshop or through experts are used to convert data to money.

Sampling Approach

With the program in place, the team wanted to evaluate the early users to judge the success and make any adjustments. The program was rolled out globally, although the United States had a bit of a head start. Although the program was rolled out to the entire workforce, the sample evaluation was limited to 198 people, composed of store associates and managers, who formed 28 teams after participating in one of 12 workshops. They each took the survey engagement before attending the workshop. A team could be as small as two people working close together on a project or as large as 10 or 12 people. The key was to have the team focused on the action plan process to improve two measures, which would be individual or team-based.

Exhibit 9-5. Data Collection Plan

Purpose of This Evaluation: <u>To show the value of engagement</u>

Program/Project: <u>Engagement</u>   Responsibility: <u>Engagement team</u>   Date: _____

Level	Broad Program Objective(s)	Measures	Data Collection Method or Instruments	Data Sources	Timing	Responsibilities
1	**SATISFACTION/PLANNED ACTION** Participants will rate the following reactions: • The program is important to my success • The program is important to HFS success • Content is relevant to our needs • The technology was user-friendly • The program was easy to follow • The classroom session was a good investment of my time • I would recommend this program to others • I will use the content in my work • The action plan was valuable	• 4 out of 5 on a 5-point scale	• Questionnaire	• Participants	• 2 to 4 months from start of program • Most items collected at the end of workshop	• Employee engagement team
2	**LEARNING** Demonstrate successful knowledge of the following skill sets: • My role • My team • My customer • My responsibilities • My career • My leadership • My community	• Rating of 4 out of 5 on a 5-point scale • Yes or No	• Questioning • Observation	• Participants • Facilitator	• At the end of the e-learning • At the end of the workshop	• Program designer • Facilitator

EXHIBIT 9-5. Data Collection Plan (continued)

Level	Broad Program Objective(s)	Measures	Data Collection Method or Instruments	Data Sources	Timing	Responsibilities
3	**APPLICATION AND IMPLEMENTATION** Participants will: • Complete the action plan items within four months • Use the coach • Use the engagement portal • Use the seven engagement concepts • Use the engagement frequently • Achieve success with engagement	• Checklist • 4 out of 5 on a 5-point scale • 4 out of 5 on a 5-point scale • 4 out of 5 on a 5-point scale	• Action Plan • Questionnaire	• Participants	• 2 months	• Engagement team
4	**BUSINESS IMPACT** Participants will make improvements in at least two of the following measures: • New customers • Increased sales with current customers • Voluntary turnover • Store profit margin • Product returns • Inventory shrinkage • Store expenses • Customer complaints • Compliance discrepancies • NPS • Customer loyalty	• Definitions vary with the measure	• Action plan	• Participants	• 4 months after workshop	• Engagement team
5	**ROI 20%**	Comments:				

EXHIBIT 9-6. ROI Analysis Plan

Purpose of This Evaluation: To show the value of engagement

Program/Project: Engagement

Responsibility: Engagement team

Date:

Data Items (Usually Level 4)	Methods for Isolating the Effects of the Program/Process	Methods of Converting Data to Monetary Values	Cost Categories	Intangible Benefits	Communication Targets for Final Report	Other Influences/ Issues During Application	Comments
At least two measures selected by team	Participant's estimate	Standard values or expert input	• Initial analysis and assessment • Development of solutions • Implementation and application • Salaries and benefits for engagement team • Salaries and benefits for coordination time • Salaries and benefits for participants' times • Salaries and benefits for coaches' time • Program materials • Travel, lodging, and meals • Use of facilities • Administrative support and overhead • Evaluation and reporting	• Teamwork • Career satisfaction • Net promoter score • Community image • Reputation • Brand • Customer loyalty • Reduction in carbon emissions • Community impact	• Top executives • Regional store managers • HR team • Participants • Engagement team • Prospective participants		

RESULTS

Exhibit 9-7 shows the data collection responses from all the planned data collection. The first part was the preprogram engagement survey, which targeted 210 people, of which 198 were in the first workshops. The pre-survey received 202 responses, representing 96 percent. During the workshop, several data sets were collected. First, reaction to the program and the concepts was collected, with 183 people providing the data (92 percent). For learning, the facilitator observed 198 associates and managers, and a subjective assessment was done to make sure the individuals were grasping the concepts and able to use them comfortably in their discussions.

In their workshop, the managers had more practice with the skills and were also observed by the facilitator, with a 100 percent "pass" rate. Although the end of each e-learning module captured some learning data, a questionnaire was used to capture learning data in the context of employee capability. While 160 of the associates received the survey, 147 of them completed it, for a response rate of 92 percent.

Two months later the post-program engagement survey was collected using the workshop participants as the target group. All 198 participants were sent the engagement survey and 169 people responded, for an 85 percent response rate. In addition, the same group received another questionnaire, which asked a few questions about the process; 174 people responded, representing 88 percent. Action plans were developed by 28 teams, with a total of 192 people participating. (Apparently, six people failed to connect with a team.) Four months later, 23 teams reported data with completed plans and five were either not available or did not provide the data. Thus, action plan data from 162 employees (84 percent) were provided, which represents 82 percent of the teams.

Exhibit 9-7. Data Collection Responses

Level	Description	Method	Audience	Sent	Received	% Received
0	Input	Preprogram Survey	All	210	202	96%
1	Reaction	Questionnaire	All	198	183	92%
2	Learning	Observation	All	198	198	100%
		Observation	Managers	38	38	100%
		Questionnaire	Associates	160	147	92%
3	Application	Post-Program Survey	All	198	169	85%
		Questionnaire	All	198	174	88%
4	Impact	Action Plan	Teams	192 (28 teams)	162 (23 teams)	82%

Level 1 (Reaction) Results

Exhibit 9-8 shows how participants reacted to the program based on the data captured at the end of the workshop. This provided an opportunity for employees and their managers to clarify their reactions and provide responses. The group's average reaction met or exceeded expectations (four out of five on a five-point scale). A total of 183 responded to this questionnaire, representing a 96 percent response rate. The responses from managers and employees were similar and are reported together. The technology effectiveness question (question 4) had a lower-than-expected result, which may reflect several technology glitches; for example, some participants had difficulty following the different modules and processes. Otherwise, the reaction to the program was very good, with "intent to use" being the star measure.

EXHIBIT 9-8. Reaction Results

	Average Reaction
The program is important to my success	4.4
The program is important to HFS's success	4.4
The content is relevant to our needs	4.4
The technology was user friendly	3.8
The classroom session was a good investment of my time	4.1
I would recommend this program to others	4.2
The program was easy to follow	3.9
I will use the content in my work	4.5
The action plan was valuable	4.2

Using a 5-point scale (n = 183)

Level 2 (Learning) Results

The first measure of learning was the observation of the skill practices. Because employees had to repeat practices if the skills were unsatisfactory, all participants scored satisfactory, as reported by the facilitators (all passed). For associates, role plays were minimal, whereas they were significant for managers. Additional learning results were connected by having the participants rate the extent to which they have the capability to use those skills. This observation was completed during the workshop, and a total of 147 people responded. "My Leadership" and "My Community" received the lowest ratings, which is understandable because some employees were uncomfortable with leadership issues and involvement in their community.

Exhibit 9-9. Learning Results

	Average reaction
I am capable of using "My Role" concepts	4.8
I am capable of using "My Team" concepts	4.7
I am capable of using "My Customer" concepts	4.4
I am capable of using "My Responsibilities" concepts	4.1
I am capable of using "My Career" concepts	4.1
I am capable of using "My Leadership" concepts	3.9
I am capable of using "My Community" concepts	3.8

Using a 5-point scale (n = 147)

Level 3 (Application) Results

Exhibit 9-10 shows the application results collected two to four months after the workshop. It begins with the percent of teams completing action plans (82 percent), which was a very high number considering the detail involved in the actual planning process. The percent using coaching was a little less than expected, as well as those using the engagement portal. Although no objectives were set for portal use or coaching use, it was expected that almost all participants would use both. Pre- and post-engagement surveys (which each had 25 questions) showed gains, although the engagement skill sets were already there for many participants. The score of 3.6 is close to where it needs to be for success (four out of five). On the post-assessment, the results moved to a 4.5 for total skill assessment. The extent of use result just met the objective and was lower for frequency and success with use. The results shown are for a composite of all seven modules. The most valuable, least valuable, and most difficult engagement skills were what would be expected for this kind of process: career, leadership, and community, respectively.

Exhibit 9-10. Application Results

	Percent responding
Percent completing action plans	82%
Percent using the manager in a coaching	51%
Percent using the engagement	61%
Average for engagement survey (8 skills): (24 Survey Items)	
Pre	3.61
Post	4.52
For engagement skills—self assessment on a composite of seven modules	
Extent of use	4.3
Frequency of use	4.1
Success with use	4.2

Using a 5-point scale

Barriers and Enablers

Exhibit 9-11 shows the barriers to use. As expected, there were not many barriers. The greatest barrier was not enough time, which was anticipated given the time constraints for the e-learning and virtual modules. The other noted barriers were minor, ranging from technology to lack of support, although lack of support was in the acceptable range.

EXHIBIT 9-11. Barriers to Use

	Percent responding
Not enough time to make it work	21%
Program was too comprehensive	14%
Lack of support from regional manager	8%
Technology issues	9%
Doesn't fit the culture	7%
Too difficult to use the concepts	6%
Other	8%

Also, as expected, the enablers were present with many of the participants, as shown in Exhibit 9-12. This is encouraging because of the high use of the skill and follow-through on the action plans. The greatest enabler was the value of the engagement concepts, which was relevant to managers and employees. Following this was manager support. However, it was anticipated that the engagement portal would be rated higher than it was.

EXHIBIT 9-12. Enablers to Success

	Percent responding
Valuable concepts	77%
Manager support	71%
Motivation	62%
Easy to use	52%
Team support	31%
Engagement portal	24%
Customer feedback	19%
Community response	12%
Other	21%

Level 4 (Impact) Results

Exhibit 9-13 shows the impact results in terms of the particular measures chosen by teams. Each team was asked to select at least two measures to improve using the engagement skills, concepts, and competencies in the program. By design, the measure should have a monetary value attached to it (or one that could be located easily). This eliminated the community measures, NPS, and customer loyalty.

Exhibit 9-13. Impact Results

Business Measures Selected	Number	Percent selecting
New accounts	11	21%
Increased revenue from current customers	9	17%
Store profit margin	7	13%
Voluntary turnover	6	12%
Product returns	4	8%
Inventory shrinkage	3	6%
Direct store expenses	3	6%
Customer complaints	2	4%
Compliance discrepancies	2	4%
Other	5	10%

Each team was required to select at least two measures.
A few managers selected three measures. (n = 52)

As expected, the most often used measure was acquiring new customers. HFS provided mechanisms to reach out to individuals who were not current clients, which was important for the teams, who selected that measure for improvement 21 percent of the time. The number 2 measure was increasing sales with current customers—including taking extra effort to up-sell, cross-sell, and entice current customers to visit the store more often and provide excellent service to make them buy more (17 percent of the managers selected this measure).

Increasing store profit margins was the next measure (13 percent), which was improved by controlling expenses, limiting waste, and avoiding price discounting or the need to give discounts to compensate for problems. Staff turnover came in fourth with 12 percent, although turnover at HFS is lower than a typical retail store. Product returns were reduced and 8 percent selected this measure. Returns occur when customers aren't fully satisfied with the product they have purchased or the product has not lived up to expectations. Good customer service can reduce returns. Inventory shrinkage was another important measure for consideration with 6 percent. Controlling costs and reducing customer complaints were the next two measures (6 percent and 4 percent, respectively). Finally, some managers addressed the compliance discrepancies measure (4 percent). There were several other miscellaneous measures that were either unique to a particular store or an unusual problem that was not one of the key measures. A few ambitious managers selected more than two measures.

Isolating the Effects of the Program

To have a credible analysis, initial steps had to be taken to isolate the effects of the program from other influences. Given the sales and marketing metrics that were used, many other factors will affect these measures, which often leaves a program like this with only a minor part of the improvement. While several processes were considered, such as setting up a control group or using simple trend line analysis, the team settled on using estimates from the participants.

The estimates were collected on the action-planning document (see Exhibit 9-14, on the next page), with explanation in the workshop as to what was involved in the estimate and how important the issue was to the final analysis. In addition, the estimate was adjusted for error using a confidence estimate. Research has shown that estimates taken from credible people in a nonthreatening way are accurate and conservative.

Converting Data to Money

To determine the monetary benefits, each individual data item has to be converted for use to money. This has to be profit-added, costs reduced, or costs avoided. Exhibit 9-15 shows the measures that are driven in this program, along with the monetary value. These values were provided to the participants in the program, which means that it took almost no effort on their part to locate and use them in their action plan.

For new accounts, the marketing analytics section calculated the value based on the profit from the customer over the lifetime of the customer. In essence, if the customer stays active with the company for an average of five years, the company will make $650 in profit during that time. For the second measure, sales to current customers, the store operating profit margin is the value-add, which is averaging 20 percent.

Exhibit 9-15. Converting Data to Money

Data Item	Value
New account	$650
Sales with existing customers	20% margin
Store profit margin	All is value-add profit
Staff turnover	60% of annual salary
Product returns	10% of average sale
Inventory shrinkage	All is value-add profit
Store expenses	All is value-add profit
Customer complaints	$500 per complaint
Compliance discrepancies	$500-1500

EXHIBIT 9-14. Action Plan Focused on Obtaining New Accounts

Team: _____   Manager: _____   Engagement Team: _____

Objective: Increase new accounts by 20%   Evaluation Period: Jan – April

Improvement Measure: Monthly Sales   Current Performance: 118 for team of six   Target Performance: 142

Action Steps		Analysis
1. Use engagement concepts	Routinely	A. What is the unit of measure? One new account
2. Meet with team to discuss issues, concerns, opportunities.	Jan. 31	
3. Encourage store visitors to go to website	Feb.2	B. What is the value (cost) of one unit? $650
4. Review customer NPS data—search for trends and patterns.	Feb. 5	C. How did you arrive at this value? Market Research
5. Meet with current customers to identify potential customers.	Feb. 8	D. How much did the measure change during the evaluation period (monthly value)? 29
6. Develop a plan for use of free samples.	Feb.10	E. What other factors could have contributed to this improvement? Customer referral or new promotion
7. Provide recognition to clients with long tenure. Ask for referral.	Feb 15	F. What percent of this change was actually caused by this program? 40%
8. Schedule appreciation actions for key clients. Ask for referrals.	Feb.17	G. What level of confidence do you place on the above information? (100% = Certainty and 0% = No confidence) 80%
9. Follow up with each discussion to discuss improvement and plan other action.	Routinely	
10. Monitor improvement; provide support when appropriate.	March 15	
Intangible benefits: Client satisfaction, loyalty		Comments: Excellent program

The store profit margin is already converted to money and any increases in value are benefits. The staff turnover figure comes from external studies about the cost of turnover for the retail industry—it totals 60 percent of annual pay and is accepted within the company as a credible, conservative number. This figure includes all costs of recruiting selection and onboarding, as well as the disruption cost of voluntary turnover. The customer care center uses 10 percent of the average sale to calculate product return. The cost is based on assumptions that the items may be damaged and cannot be resold, the items always need to be restocked, and an adjustment may need to be made. Inventory shrinkage is reported as money lost because of lost inventory.

Store expenses are direct cost reductions and are value-added directly into the calculation. Customer complaints come from the customer care center and are investigated locally, regionally, and globally, if needed. The group uses a model that estimates a cost of $500 per complaint. This assumes the time to address the complaint, the cost of satisfying the customer (which sometimes includes waiving part or all of the charge), and the ill will caused by the complaint.

The cost of a compliance discrepancy varies depending on the compliance and issue. These involve store compliance regulations from the city, county, state, and federal government. It could involve safety, environment, labor, or other issues. The team was asked to contact the compliance department for the estimate.

Monetary Benefits

When changes in the impact measures identified in Exhibit 9-13 are adjusted for the effect of the program and converted to monetary values using the data in Exhibit 9-15, the monetary benefits are developed. The improvement is different from one store to another—23 teams comprising 162 people completed the action plans and every team's task was to improve at least two measures. Unfortunately, five teams did not provide an action plan in four months. Although would be helpful to find out what happened, in terms of the analysis there is a very specific rule for addressing missing data: Guiding Principle 6 indicates that missing data get a zero in the process. Thus, the total benefits are adjusted based on the 23 teams and 162 individuals who provided data, but the cost is based on all 28 teams and 193 employees.

Exhibit 9-16 shows a one-page sample of 12 pages of data showing the improvements connected to this program. While it only represents 12 measures, it illustrates the variety of data represented in the program, and shows how the adjustments are made. Three other tables complete the 52 measures for the 23 teams.

Next, the first-year value of this measure is developed using the data conversion numbers in Exhibit 9-15. Although there could be some argument to suggest that this is a long-term program and that the benefits should be considered for a longer period, only the first year of benefits are calculated. This means that after the impact occurred, the amount was extrapolated for the entire year. Some may suggest that this is not credible because the data might not continue at that level for the entire first year.

However, when considering that the vast majority of the team members will still be in their jobs the second, third, and perhaps even fourth year, there should be some benefit from this program as long as they are in that job. A multiyear benefit also could be used. However, because it is possible to take the prework, attend the workshop, and work the virtual process in a few weeks, this was considered a short-term solution, so only one year of impact was used. This is to be conservative, which is reflected in Guiding Principle 9. Exhibit 9-16 shows the monetary value for one year.

The contribution factor is the allocation to this program, because the team members provided a particular percent of the improvement that is directly related to the program. The next column is the confidence, which reflects the error in the allocation. Following the process, using Guiding Principle 7, the three values are multiplied to provide an adjusted value. When these are calculated for all 162 participants, including both measures, the total is 52 measures improved by at least some amount. With all of these totaled, the improvement is based on 52 measures valued to be $1,386,024.

The Costs

Exhibit 9-17 shows the costs allocated to this program, some of which were prorated just to this sample size. For example, the needs assessment cost was estimated to be approximately $25,000, which includes reviews, focus groups, and interviews. This amount involves the up-front analysis necessary to decide on the specific need for this program. This value is divided by the total employees to yield a cost per employee, and then multiplied by 192, which is the total in the sample.

The most significant cost was the development. Some content was purchased from a major supplier, an outside production company produced the videos, and other content was developed under contract with freelancers or by the L&D team. In total, the development and production costs for the materials and videos totaled $425,000. Separately, the development of the two workshops cost $35,000.

The content for the engagement portal was developed for approximately $75,000, and developing the seven e-learning modules was about another $84,000. These costs were prorated over the 40,000 employees to develop a cost per participant. The total costs allocated to this sample of 192 represent the cost per participant multiplied by 192. Exhibit 9-17 shows the prorated costs for these items. The cost of equipment and components were estimated to be around $12 per participant.

The coach's time was allocated at a half day per participant, because not all participants used their coach, and others used the coach for more than half a day total. For participants, the costs were calculated by their time for a day, the time away from work for the e-learning modules, and any other virtual activities. A total of three days of time was used. Most participants also required a travel expense, although minor. The cost of trainers, facilitation and coordination, and facilities and refreshments were easily available.

Exhibit 9-16. Business Impact Data

Team	Annualized Improvement ($Value)	Measures	Other Factors	Contribution Estimate From Program	Confidence Estimate	Adjusted ($ Value)
1	142,400 Profit	Sales—Current	4	30%	60%	25,632
2	178,000 Profit	New Accounts	3	40%	85%	60,520
3	218,000 Costs	Voluntary Turnover	2	50%	70%	76,300
4	72,500 Profit	Sales—Current	3	40%	80%	23,200
5	68,000 Costs	Product Returns	1	70%	65%	30,940
6	226,200 Profit	New Accounts	2	40%	80%	72,384
7	7,000 Costs	Compliance	0	100%	100%	7,000
8	65,000 Costs	Store Expense	0	100%	95%	61,750
9	26,000 Costs	Inventory	2	40%	80%	8,320
10	21,400 Costs	Customer Complaints	2	40%	70%	5,992
11	99,000 Costs	Turnover	2	30%	70%	20,790
12	52,300 Profits	Store Profit	3	40%	85%	17,782

Total this team $410,610

Three other tables $975,414

Total $1,386,610

157

Exhibit 9-18. Program Costs Summary

Needs assessment (prorated over all employees)	
$25,000 ÷ 40,000 employees = 0.625 × 192	$120
Program development and video production costs (prorated over all sessions)	
$425,000 ÷ 40,000 = 10.625 × 192	2,040
Content development for workshops (prorated over all sessions)	
$35,000 ÷ 40,000 = 0.875 × 192	168
Engagement portal (prorated over all sessions)	
$75,000 ÷ 40,000 = 1.875 × 192	360
E-learning programs (prorated over all sessions)	
$84,000 ÷ 40,000 = 2.1 × 192	403
E-learning components used by participants	
$12 × 192	2,304
Program materials	
$35 × 192	6,720
Travel and lodging: participants	
$390 × 192	74,880
Facilitation and coordination	
$6,000 × 12 days of facilitation, trainer, and coordination	72,000
Facilities and refreshments	
12 days at $220 per day	2,640
Participants salaries plus benefits	
$734 × 192	140,928
Coaches' salaries plus benefits	
$520 × 192	99,840
Overhead	4,200
ROI evaluation	
$40,000	40,000
Total	**$446,603**

In addition, an overhead cost for the total employee engagement team, including the L&D leadership not directly involved in the program, was estimated to be $4,200. The cost of the evaluation, which comprised the planning, data instrument design, data collection, analysis report writing, and briefings, was $40,000, including the cost of the briefings with travel. With all costs included, the total as indicated in Exhibit 9-17 is $446,603.

ROI Calculation

When the total monetary benefits from Exhibit 9-16 are compared with the total fully loaded costs from Exhibit 9-17, the calculations are as follows:

$$BCR = \frac{\$1,386,024}{\$446,603} = 3.1$$

$$ROI = \frac{\$1,386,024 - \$446,603}{\$446,603} \times 100 = 210\%$$

This is a very impressive ROI that greatly exceeds the objective of 20 percent. For every dollar invested in this program, it is returned plus another $2.10 in monetary benefits.

Intangible Benefits

The list of the intangibles connected with this project included teamwork, career satisfaction, net promoter score, customer loyalty, community image, reputation, brand, and reduction in carbon emissions. The participants were asked to indicate the extent to which these intangibles were influenced by the program. In order for a suggested intangible benefit to be included on this list, at least 10 percent of participants had to identify the influence as at least three out of five on a five-point scale. These intangibles represent an important data set for executives. If they were converted to monetary value, there would be even more value from this program and a higher ROI.

Credibility of the Data

When employee engagement is connected to the business in a program like this, there are always questions about the credibility of data. Here is what makes these data credible:

1. The business impact, which drives the ROI, represented actual store measures. They can be identified directly to the store and tracked and validated if necessary.
2. The participants selected the measures that were important to them with input from their immediate manager.

3. Participants had a desire to improve the measure, and took ownership in the program as they connected the skills of engagement to those important measures.

4. For participants who did not provide data (five teams in this case), there was an assumption that they received no value from the program. In reality, some of these individuals changed stores, either through promotion or transfer, and actually gained value despite not completing the project. However, the conservative approach is to use zero for them.

5. Only one year of improvement was recognized in the calculation. In reality, the significant change in engagement, which was validated with the data collection at Level 3, should provide value for a second, third, and even fourth year. However, to be conservative, only the first year was used.

6. All the costs were tabulated including time away from work. Some of these costs are debatable, but to be credible, every cost category was included.

7. Using participant estimates to isolate the effects of the program was not the most favored approach, but it is credible. The estimation was collected in a nonthreatening, unbiased way, and was adjusted for error.

8. A balanced profile of financial and nonfinancial, quantitative and qualitative data was presented. This provided executives with a great data set to make decisions about future implementation of the program.

COMMUNICATION OF RESULTS

With the results in hand, the data were communicated to the groups according to the communication plan. First, a live briefing was conducted with top executives and those responsible for the implementation of the program. In addition, briefings were conducted with regional executives during normal meetings and with the HR team. A three-page summary was sent to all store managers. The participants received a summary of the results shortly after they submitted them, as well as a summary of the changes made as a result of the program.

Based on the briefings with the executive team, the following adjustments were made:

- Improvements were made to make the technology easier and more reliable.
- The role of the participant's manager was strengthened to make sure that proper measures were selected and any needed support was provided.
- The role of the coach was diminished.
- Some efforts were taken to strengthen the link between the engagement survey and the rest of the program. There was concern that the engagement survey was not tightly integrated into the program.
- Another group of participants (teams) would be monitored in six months to ensure that the programs were still working.

QUESTIONS FOR DISCUSSION

1. How did the company's new definition of engagement influence the design of the employee engagement program?
2. Discuss the importance of getting participants committed to provide quality data.
3. Critique the evaluation, design, and method of data collection.
4. Is this case study credible? Explain.
5. How can this type of process be used to build support for programs in the future?
6. How can the outcomes of engagement be linked to your organization's business objectives?

REFERENCE

Hsieh, T. 2010. *Delivering Happiness: A Path to Profits, Passion, and Purpose.* New York: Business Plus.

10

Measuring the ROI of a New Engagement-Based Selection Process
International Premium Hotel Group

Jack J. Phillips and Patti P. Phillips

T his case was prepared to serve as a basis for discussion rather than to illustrate either effective or ineffective administrative and management practices. All names, dates, places, and organizations have been disguised at the request of the author or organization.

Abstract

This case study shows the ROI in a new comprehensive selection process, which includes a new recruiting source, instruments to measure the engagement of candidates, a simulation to measure customer engagement approaches, and a realistic job preview. This upscale hotel chain needed new employees to fit into their engagement culture and be prepared to provide the ultimate customer experience. After experiencing problems with turnover of new employees when they could not adjust to the engagement culture, the recruiting and selection system was changed to include improvements in retention, the time to employ new candidates, employee performance, and guest satisfaction.

BACKGROUND

International Premium Hotels (IPH) owns more than 70 upscale hotels operating in 12 countries. Through its different brands, IPH prides itself on providing excellent guest satisfaction delivered by employees who have superb hospitality skills. The hotel business is a very competitive market and guest satisfaction is a critical measure. IPH charges a premium price, and for that, it wants to offer a premium service. Providing a less-than-desired service level will affect the company's image, ultimately leading to a reduction in revenue. At the same time, IPH must also be efficient and manage costs within appropriate ranges.

The Situation

The cost of high staff turnover in the first 60 days of employment has been increasing hotel costs. Management is concerned that the quality of the new staff is not where it should be in terms of being engaged with the work and customers. The IPH executives asked the HR team to experiment with new recruiting and selection processes to decrease the turnover of employees early in their tenure while also improving guest satisfaction and employee performance. The first pilot program would be for 24 hotels in the United States. If the concept proved effective, it would be adapted to different cultures in other countries and implemented globally.

The first step was for the IPH HR staff to examine why the company was facing unusually high turnover in the first 60 days. Focus groups were conducted using a nominal group technique to arrive at the cause of turnover (Phillips and Edwards 2009). The team found that the top reasons for early turnover were that employees were:
- not adapting to the engagement culture
- lacking hospitality experience
- not providing the level of engagement needed
- in a job that wasn't what they had expected.

The definition of the turnover measure is avoidable turnover. In addition to voluntary turnovers, other turnovers could be avoided if actions were taken to prevent terminations. These could be prevented through counseling or improved selection processes.

SOLUTION

Armed with the information from the focus groups, the following solutions were developed and approved:
- Change the recruitment efforts to a website and recruiting source that would attract experienced hospitality candidates.
- Administer an engagement preference instrument that matches the candidate's value systems with the hotel's value systems.
- Conduct customer engagement exercises where the candidates would view a variety of videos and make a decision about what to do in each case. The assessment is designed to pinpoint a candidate's attitude toward customer engagement and customer satisfaction.
- Provide a realistic job preview. The last stage in the selection process assigns a new candidate to a brief rotational process lasting about two hours to

provide a sense of the customer engagement culture in the hotel. This was designed to have candidates self-select out of the process if they are not comfortable with the engagement culture.

Recruiting Method

The first solution is changing the recruiting method, which involved using a new website that serves as a job match for the hospitality industry. Employers can advertise jobs and include the requirements and necessary qualifications on the site. Candidates can apply and provide background information; they are forwarded to the company if their credentials meet the requirements the company requires. IPH had previously used local recruiting sources, job ads, and other online services to recruit the candidates. This new website was expected to provide more experienced candidates for the hospitality industry.

Engagement

The second solution is an engagement fit instrument that checked validity and reliability. The instrument assesses what candidates want and need at work and compares them with the engagement profile of successful employees to see if their profiles match. If a profile doesn't match, the candidate should be rejected. The data show that this instrument can prevent early turnover because it ensures a proper match between the engagement culture of the organization and the work values of the candidate. A partial listing of the statements candidates agree or disagree with using a five-point scale includes:

1. I prefer to work in a stress-free environment.
2. My work is not successful until the customer is satisfied.
3. I work best when I can control my schedule.
4. I take full responsibility for my results.
5. There is a limit to what we can do to satisfy a customer.
6. I work best in a supportive team environment.
7. A customer referral is more important than having a satisfied customer.
8. My work must be important.
9. My pay increases should be in proportion to my contribution.
10. I need to be recognized for my work.
11. I prefer individual rewards to team rewards.
12. I need clear expectations for my work.
13. Every customer service issue can be resolved.
14. I need opportunities to grow at work.
15. Quality of work is more important than quantity of work.
16. I need routine feedback on my progress.

Customer Service

The third solution is a customer service simulation, where the candidates view a variety of customer service videos and are asked to indicate a course of action. The situations require a person to use judgment, knowing when and how to respond to a customer as they are empowered to take that action. At the same time, they must not be too extreme with customer wishes. IPH struggles with this issue because it wants customer service staff to be empowered to take care of the customer at almost any cost, but know when the requests and issues are on the unreasonable side.

Realistic Job Preview

A fourth solution is the realistic job preview. This is based on the assumption that individuals need to see the actual job or some parts of it in operation. That way they can self-select out of the process if it isn't a good fit. In this situation, the individual observes as many issues as possible in a two-hour period in a real-life setting. This is not a new concept and has a history of minimizing early turnovers.

Exhibit 10-1 shows the concept of this new selection process, where the pool of applicants is initially very broad but then the hospitality source reduces that number considerably. The engagement instrument narrows it even more, and the customer service exercise even reduces it further. Finally the realistic job preview allows some participants to self-select out of the process. The result is the eligible list of candidates.

Exhibit 10-1. New Components of Recruiting and Selection Process

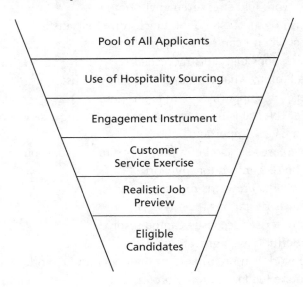

Pool of All Applicants

Use of Hospitality Sourcing

Engagement Instrument

Customer Service Exercise

Realistic Job Preview

Eligible Candidates

Exhibit 10-2 shows the selection system and what has been added. The process is comprehensive, systematic, and can easily be administered by each hotel's HR staff. The goal is to process as many qualified candidates through the system as quickly as possible, ensuring that those candidates fit in the organization properly and remain for a longer period of time.

Exhibit 10-2. The Revised Recruiting and Selection System

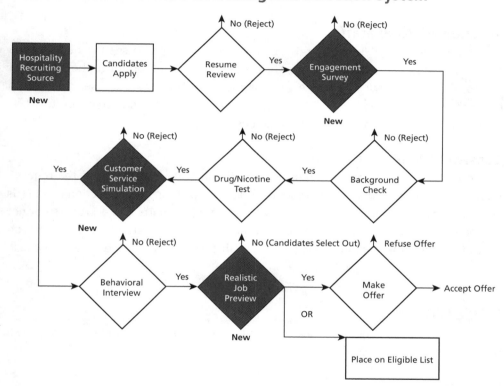

IMPLEMENTATION CHALLENGES

Cost

The new processes will increase the cost of recruiting and selection. The challenge is to keep these costs to a minimum while weighing the cost versus the monetary benefit of the change. This situation creates the desire to conduct the ROI analysis.

Time to Start

This new process must be implemented efficiently so that it does not add to the time to start, which is an important measure at the hotel. The time to start is a measure of time from the point that a particular job opening has been identified and a requisition has been signed to the day when the new candidate is on the job. Time to start is currently averaging 30 days and this measure needs to be at the same number (or less), even though the extra steps of the new system are extending the selection process.

Reaction to Hotel Staff

It is important for the HR staff and executives at each hotel to see the need for the change in recruitment and selection. They must see it as important to the success of the hotel and necessary to enhance guest satisfaction. They must also see the need to make the change based on the current level of performance and retention, which is linked to the selection of improper candidates.

Consistent Implementation

This process must be administered consistently and efficiently. One of the requirements of having a valid selection system is that the recruiting and selection process is always consistent. There is no option to administer some parts of the process but not others. For example, the same amount of time should be allocated for the realistic job previews each time a candidate participates in this step. But candidates must also proceed efficiently through the selection system.

OBJECTIVES

The program's objectives are critical to maintain the focus on the solutions. The objectives are set at five levels.

Reaction

Based on the analysis and implementation issues described already, the following objectives were developed for reaction. After implementing this program, the HR recruiting and selecting team will see this program as important to the company's success, important to guest satisfaction, necessary for recruiting qualified candidates, and one they intend to implement properly.

Learning

After initiating this project, the stakeholders will be able to properly use the new recruiting source, the engagement assessment instrument, a simulation on customer service, and the realistic job preview.

Application

When the project is implemented:

- The new recruiting source will be used appropriately and routinely to attract candidates.
- The engagement survey will be administered timely and consistently for each applicant.
- The customer service simulation will be administered under consistent conditions.
- The job preview will be implemented each time under the same conditions.

Impact

After the program is fully implemented:

- The avoidable turnover rate (annualized) in the first three months of employment will be reduced from 28 percent to 18 percent, which is a reduction of 10 percentage points.
- Guest satisfaction will be maintained or improved.
- The performance of new employees will be improved one half of one point on a five-point scale.
- The time to start measure will not exceed 30 days.
- Employee job engagement will improve.

ROI

The ROI objective for this project is set at 20 percent, which is the minimum acceptable performance.

DATA COLLECTION

Exhibit 10-3 shows a data collection plan for this project. First a questionnaire will be administered to the HR team that is involved in the recruiting, testing, assessment, and selection processes. This questionnaire will capture reaction and learning data three weeks after the new system is implemented, using self-assessment input that explores any issues that are surfacing at this point. Two months after implementation, another questionnaire will be administered to ensure that all the four processes are operating properly.

For Level 4 assessments, the source of turnover and time to start data will be in the records. The rest of the impact measures will be in a questionnaire administered in four months. By then, the impact should materialize and this questionnaire will also be used to isolate the effects of this program on the impact data. Exhibit 10-4 shows the data integration by level.

Exhibit 10-3. Data Collection Plan for the New Recruiting and Selection System

Program/Project: <u>Recruiting/Selection Project</u>   Responsibility: _____   Date: _____

Level	Broad Program Objective(s)	Measures	Data Collection Method/Instruments	Data Sources	Timing	Responsibilities
1	**SATISFACTION/PLANNED ACTION** • Participants must see it is important to hotel success • Participants must see it is important to guest satisfaction • Participants must see it is necessary to recruit • Participants must intend to use	• 4 out of 5 on a 5-point scale	• Questionnaire	• HR team	• Just after implementation (3 weeks)	• HR team
2	**LEARNING** Participants must be able to describe and use: • recruiting source • engagement instrument • customer service simulation • realistic job preview	• 4 out of 5 on a 5-point scale	• Questionnaire	• HR team	• Just after implementation (3 weeks)	• HR team

3	**APPLICATION/ IMPLEMENTATION**					
	The use of: • Recruiting source • Engagement assessment • Customer service simulation • Realistic job preview	• 4 out of 5 on a 5-point scale	• Questionnaire • Interview • Performance monitoring	• HR team • HR system records	• 2 months after implementation	• HR team
4	**BUSINESS IMPACT**					
	• Reduce early turnover by 10 percentage points • Enhance guest satisfaction • Time to start will not exceed 15 days • Enhance employee performance • Enhance employee engagement	• % leaving (avoidable) • 4 of 5 on a 5-point scale	• Performance monitoring • Questionnaire	• HR system records • HR team	• 4 months after implementation	• HR team
5	**ROI** 20%	Comments:				

Exhibit 10-4. Data Summary and Integration

	Reaction	Learning	Application	Impact	Barriers and Enablers	Costs
Questionnaire Just After Launch (3 weeks)	X	X				
Questionnaire After Launch (2 months)			X		X	
Hotel Records (2 months)			X			
Follow-Up Questionnaire (4 months)				X		X
HR Systems (4 months)				X		X
HR Records Manager Assessment (4 months)				X		

ROI ANALYSIS PLAN

Exhibit 10-5 shows a completed ROI analysis plan. The plan starts with business impact data identified from the data collection (Level 4) and presents a method of isolation. For this project, an experimental versus control group would not be possible because immediate implementation was planned for all U.S. hotels. American executives didn't want to withhold the processes for some hotels to see the effect on the control group because they wanted to resolve the problem as quickly as possible. Hotels outside the United States would not necessarily be a good match for use as a control group because of differences in global cultures. Instead, the HR team decided to use two other methods: trend line analysis and estimates from the stakeholders involved in the process. The trend line would work only if no other new process was implemented that would affect the impact measures during the four-month period. The estimations were a fallback approach.

The team relied on an acceptable standard value for the cost of turnover to convert the data to money. Regarding guest satisfaction, the hotel had some data that indicated the monetary payoff of improving guest satisfaction, but it was not considered to be credible. Employee performance, time to start, and employee engagement were not converted to money because of the difficulty of developing a credible value.

The costs of the four new processes are fully loaded. Some additional intangibles are anticipated, which means that some information must be collected to see the extent in which these intangibles are connected to the program. The groups for communicating results are typical, with particular emphasis placed on briefing with hotel executives and providing information to the key stakeholders.

EXHIBIT 10-5. Completed ROI Analysis Plan

Purpose of This Evaluation: _____

Program/Project: Recruiting/Selection Project   **Responsibility:** _____   **Date:** _____

Data Items (Usually Level 4)	Methods for Isolating the Effects of the Program/Process	Methods of Converting Data to Monetary Values	Cost Categories	Intangible Benefits	Communication Targets for Final Report	Other Influences/ Issues During Application	Comments
Early turnover	• Trend line analysis • Participants' estimates	• Accepted value (standard)	• Needs assessment • Development • Purchase/ lease • Time for meetings/ training • Time to use the new processes • Evaluation	• Employee engagement • Time to start • Employee performance • Guest satisfaction • Reputation • Recruiting image	• Recruiting and selection team • Hotel HR managers • Hotel GMs • VP operations (corp) • VP HR (corp) • Analytics team	• This is a short-term solution; need to collect ASAP	• Implementation will be in the 24 U.S. hotels
Time to start	• Trend line analysis • Participants' estimates	N/A					

RESULTS

The results are presented by the different levels, beginning with Level 1, moving through to Level 4 and 5 analyses, and ending with intangibles.

Reaction

The reaction results are presented in Exhibit 10-6. The reaction was satisfactory except for one issue: The individuals who are involved in recruiting and selection didn't see how the project would affect guest satisfaction. Because of this, the project team put some extra effort into communications with the recruiting and selection staff to show them the connection between having a staff with a culture of customer service and guest satisfaction. Although the solution may prevent turnover in the early stages of employment, a mismatch early on in the hiring process can create problems with guest satisfaction. Having an employee with a longer tenure also provides continuity and continues to build client satisfaction.

EXHIBIT 10-6. Reaction Results

Participants Rate the Following:	Score
This program is important to hotel success	4.0
This program is important to guest satisfaction	3.2
This program is necessary for recruiting qualified candidates	4.5
This team intends to implement processes properly	4.1
	Average response = 4.0

Scale: 1 = Not at all, 2 = A little, 3 = Some, 4 = Much, 5 = Very much

Learning

Learning was obtained using a simple self-assessment on a questionnaire. The results are captured in Exhibit 10-7. The participants indicated that they could describe each of the new processes and use them properly. While there were no surprises at this level, the lowest ratings were for the customer service simulation and the realistic job previews. These were a little more complicated than the change in recruiting source and the engagement survey assessment. The excellent results at this level may be a reflection of the fact that the objectives were clearly defined.

Application

Exhibit 10-8 shows the application data and reveals that the new steps were being operated properly and consistently, except for the realistic job preview.

Exhibit 10-7. Learning Results

Participants are able to:	Score
Describe the new recruiting source and website	4.2
Use the new recruiting source and website	4.1
Use the engagement assessment	4.3
Describe the customer service simulated	3.9
Use the customer service simulated	4.0
Describe the realistic job preview process	3.8
Use the realistic job preview process	3.9
	Average response = 4.1

Scale: 1 = Not at all, 2 = Some, 3 = Moderate amount, 4 = Significant amount,
5 = Very significant amount

Exhibit 10-8. Application Results

Participants are able to:	Score
The new recruiting source is being used properly	4.2
The new recruiting source provides a steady stream of candidates	4.6
The engagement survey is administered for every candidate	4.7
The engagement survey is administered under the same conditions for each remaining candidate	4.6
The customer service simulation is administered	4.0
The customer service simulation is administered under the same conditions	4.1
The realistic job preview is administered for each remaining candidate	3.7
The realistic job preview is administered under the same conditions	3.8
The four new processes are successful	4.3

Scale: 1 = Not at all, 2 = Occasionally, 3 = Sometimes, 4 = Often, 5 = Always

Exhibit 10-9 shows the barriers to use and Exhibit 10-10 shows the enablers that support the use. The barriers reveal that the realistic job preview is a problem, with nearly 70 percent having difficulty with it. The issue is also connected to the second barrier. However, the enablers were very positive and encouraging.

Exhibit 10-9. Barriers to Effective Use

Barriers to Use	Percent Responding
The realistic job preview is difficult to execute	39%
The process takes too much time	28%
Candidates resist the two assessments	17%
It's difficult to be consistent each time	8%
Other	14%

Exhibit 10-10. Enablers to Effective Use

Enablers to Use	Percent Responding
Each step is easy to use	64%
General manager supports this process	61%
Candidates appreciate the thoroughness of our process	52%
The process is very interesting and engaging	41%
It seems to fit our engagement culture	19%
Other	17%

Exhibit 10-11 shows the efficiencies that are coming through the system with these changes. Previously, only 54 percent of applicants made it through the resume review. With this new system, 81 percent are making it through the resume review, underscoring that the recruiting source is providing more qualified candidates. Thus, out of 100 initial applications, 81 move on to the engagement assessment round, which eliminates another 29 applications. The customer service simulation drops another 10, but the realistic job preview only removes one. So in essence, this process provides better candidates in the beginning, eliminating 40 percent of applicants that would potentially have left the organization in the early stages of employment. These are impressive results, with the engagement survey having the most impact thus far. In total, 79 of the 100 candidates who applied were eliminated from consideration. The engagement survey accounted for 29 (37 percent) of the total eliminations.

Exhibit 10-11. Recruiting and Selecting Efficiencies

	For Every 100 Candidates Who Apply		
	These Remain		After
	81	81%	Resume Review
New	52	64%	Engagement Assessment
	44	84%	Background Check
	39	89%	Drug/Nicotine Test
New	29	74%	Customer Service Simulation
	22	76%	Behavioral Interviews
New	21	95%	Realistic Job Previews
	18		Make Offer
	3		Place on Eligible List
	17	94%	Accept Offer

Business Impact

The early turnover data are presented in Exhibit 10-12 for the four months prior to the program and four months after the program. As expected, the annualized turnover data are reduced.

The isolation by trend line analysis seems to work for this data set. It shows that 28 percent turnover would be expected, but after four months the actual turnover is 16 percent. The HR team indicated that the preprogram trend would probably have continued if nothing had changed in the system. More importantly, the HR team could not identify any other new influences that would have caused this improvement. Therefore it is safe to use the trend line analysis as a method of isolation.

Time to start is an important measure and Exhibit 10-13 shows the details. The program reduced the time to start to 27 days, compared with about 30 days prior to the program. However, there was already a downward trend in place the when the program started, and the projected trend line shows that time to start may have hit 27 days even without the program. This means that the program may have actually added more days to what the time to start could have been.

However, the team could not explain the downward trend on the program data, or the fact that it would have continued. Consequently, the HCA team suggested that the objective had been met.

Exhibit 10-12. Trend Line Analysis for Early Turnover

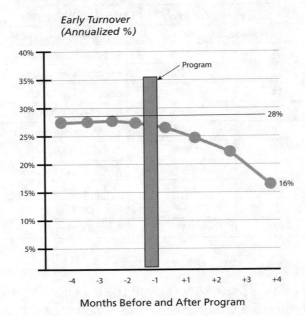

Early Turnover
(Annualized %)

Program

28%

16%

Months Before and After Program

Exhibit 10-13. Trend Line Analysis for Time to Start

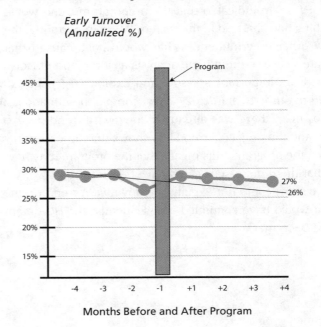

Early Turnover
(Annualized %)

Program

27%
26%

Months Before and After Program

Converting Data to Money

In total, the company was expecting to hire 255 employees in the 24 U.S. hotels during the year of this study. To calculate the cost of early turnover, the hotel had been using 40 percent of annual pay, which was a number accepted by the management team. This is for early turnover, where the investment in new employees is not as much as for longer-term employees and the loss of knowledge and experience is not very high. However, there are still up-front variable costs related to replacements, so 40 percent is a conservative number that covers the cost of recruiting, selection, employment, onboarding, and initial training before new employees become productive. It also includes the cost of the disruption and the bottlenecks caused by turnover, as well as the time involved in addressing the turnover situation. Exhibit 10-14 shows the calculation for the cost savings of the reduction in turnover.

Exhibit 10-14. Turnover Analysis

255 Employees

Turnover improvements: 28 - 16 = 12% annual

$255 \times 0.12 = 31$ employees

Average salary: $36,000

Turnover cost: 40% of salary

$36,000 \times 0.4 = 14,400$

Annual = $14,400 \times 31 = \$446,400$

The time to start decreased slightly but wasn't converted to monetary value. It is left as an intangible.

Cost

The fully loaded cost of these four solutions, including the solution and purchase instruments, is shown in Exhibit 10-15. The team was very anxious to make sure all cost were included, both direct and indirect. Some of the costs included ongoing cost in the future because these services are being used for the recruiting database, instrument, and customer service simulation. The question that surfaced was how much cost to include. In the very beginning of the project, it was determined that this would be considered a short-term solution, which means the benefits would be accumulated for one year and the early turnover would be extrapolated for an entire year when the impact was actually determined. In other words, after four months, the change in turnover rate would be extrapolated for the year to arrive at the benefits in the previous section.

A case could easily have been made for this to be a longer-term solution, which would allow two or even three years of benefits to be used. However, the team decided to use one year to increase the credibility of the data.

EXHIBIT 10-15. Fully Loaded Costs of Four Solutions

Cost of Four Solutions at 24 Hotels (Annualized and Prorated)	
Needs Assessment	
Prorated Over Five Years	$1,200
Development and Purchase	
Customer Service	15,000
Realistic Job Previews	8,000
Lease and Royalties	
Recruiting Source (Annual)	20,000
Engagement (Annual)	17,200
Customer Service Simulation (Annual)	23,500
Learning Sessions for Recruiting and Selection Team	4,300
Time to Use the Process	
Recruiting Source	Less than previous
Engagement	2,200
Administrative Issues	
Coordination, Supplies, etc.	15,800
Customer Services	4,400
Realistic Job Preview	22,000
Evaluation	4,500
Total	**$138,100**

Finally the BCR and ROI were calculated, as shown below. Monetary benefits for one year were determined to be $446,400, whereas the cost for one year of the program was $138,100.

$$BCR = \frac{\$446,000}{\$138,100} = 3.23 \text{ to } 1$$

$$ROI = \frac{\$446,400 - \$138,100}{\$138,100} \times 100 = 223\%$$

The BCR and the ROI are extremely high, making it difficult for people to accept. However, the impact data are credible because they come directly from the system. The high early turnover rate was substantially reduced, and the monetary benefits are realistic because management agreed on the cost of turnover. In addition, the program was not very expensive, particularly when considering that all of the costs for the four processes are included. The HCA team felt good that this could be defended in the communication of results.

Intangibles

This study influenced some important intangibles, with three measures that were initially identified as impact turning out to be intangibles. The time to start was not converted to money, as mentioned earlier, although there were certainly some costs avoided with improvement in that measure. Time to start was left intangible because it could not be developed credibly with a reasonable amount of resources.

The records of the individuals participating in the program were reviewed to determine employee performance. The performance was higher and slightly exceeded the requirement for one-half of one point in performance improvement. The average performance improvement rating increased from 3.8 to 4.4 on a five-point scale, where 3 is the average performance rating.

It was impossible to connect guest satisfaction directly to this group of employees. Although each hotel has guest satisfaction measures, those numbers aren't broken down by individual person or even function. However, on the questionnaire the HR team asked employees to indicate the extent to which the program had improved guest satisfaction; they were able to connect the ranking of 4.1 on a five-point scale to guest satisfaction. Other intangible measures included reputation of the hotel, brand awareness, and recruiting image (Exhibit 10-16).

Exhibit 10-16. Intangible Benefits Connected to This Program

Intangible Benefits	
Time to Start	Slight Reduction
Employee Performance	3.8–4.4
Guest Satisfaction	4.1
Recruiting Image	4.3
Brand Awareness	3.8
Hotel Reputation	3.2

Scale: 1 = No influence, 2 = Some influence, 3 = Moderate influence,
4 = Significant influence, 5 = Very significant influence

CONCLUSIONS AND RECOMMENDATIONS

This program was a success in terms of its overall connection with the impact measures. However, the realistic job preview doesn't seem to be adding value, which is addressed in the recommendation. Data collection was smooth and efficient, participation was high, barriers were minimal, and enablers were very strong. On a conservative basis, the program adds tremendous value, with most of the improvement coming from the engagement survey. The program also underscores the fact that management support was extremely high, because the HCA team was handed a problem, but not the specific solution. Although management hinted at the solution—something had to be changed in the assessment, selection, and sourcing process to stem the turnover—the specific solution was left up to the team to uncover. This works much better, instead of having the management team implement or bring a predetermined solution, only to find out later that it was not the right one. By planning for the ROI in advance, this project brought a tremendous focus on the outcome, provided for early detection of problems, and helped achieve the results that were ultimately delivered.

In terms of recommendations, the HCA team recommended that this concept be applied to hotels in other countries, but in the context of the culture of that country. This may be more expensive because of language, labor laws, and the cultures of the different countries. For some, it might not even be worth it. However, each country should be evaluated individually and at least some parts of the process should be considered.

Additionally, the realistic job preview did not have a significant effect, with only one person self-selecting out in the four months of operation results. Given the cost of this process, the difficulties the hotel HR team is having with this task, and the amount of time it takes for other hotel staff to be involved, the HR team recommended that this part be dropped from the process going forward.

COMMUNICATION PLAN

With results in hand, the first stop was the executive group. The HR team gave the U.S. hotel executives a briefing during one of their regularly scheduled meetings. This 30-minute briefing gave the team the opportunity to explain the methodology that was used, describe their results, and gain approval for their recommendations. This briefing was carefully planned and orchestrated and was successful in meeting the agenda and achieving its purposes. Beyond that, a summary and full report was sent to the HR team involved in the project. This was followed with a webinar briefing, which used the same set of slides as the executive group briefing. In addition, all the hotel general managers were given a summary, a complete report, and a webinar on the results, with opportunities for Q&A. This hour and a half session accomplished the same goals as the executive briefing, but included a little more detail about operational issues at the hotel.

In addition, the team wrote a brief article for the employee newsletter explaining the study, what was done, and results that were achieved. A complete study was also made available to the HR managers at all the hotels in the United States and internationally. A webinar was offered to this complete group and was conducted in two sessions, one with the U.S. HR managers, and the other with those outside the United States, with some discussion around the applicability and feasibility of the same process in their country.

Finally, a brief paragraph of this study was included in the quarterly financial report that was released the quarter following the executive briefing. This was designed to alert investors of the progress being made to make the organization more successful in terms of guest satisfaction and controlling cost.

LESSONS LEARNED

The lessons learned from this program are very straightforward:

- It is best to have a problem to work with so the team can find the right solution. This is in contrast to many requests when the solution is brought to the HR team.
- The decision to measure the impact and ROI was made early, at the time of the analysis. This helped in planning the study, making it more focused, and keeping the attention on results throughout the implementation. This approach actually enhanced the results that were achieved.
- Excellent support of the management group made it successful. The hotel general managers saw the problem, knew it was expensive, and were pleased to see the solution.
- This type of analysis does take a little bit of time, but when it is all considered, it is worth it. The extra efforts are actually necessary steps in the process.

QUESTIONS FOR DISCUSSION

1. Is this study credible? Please explain.
2. Are there other potential solutions to this problem? Please explain.
3. Critique the data collection. Are there other ways to collect data? If so, explain.
4. What others ways could be used to isolate the effects of the program?
5. Could the effects of the engagement be isolated from other parts of the solution? If so, how could this be accomplished?
6. Could the ROI from the engagement survey be calculated? If so, how?
7. Should this be a long-term or short-term solution? Explain.
8. Could you defend this study with your executives? Please explain.

REFERENCE

Phillips, J.J., and L. Edwards. 2009. *Managing Talent Retention: An ROI Approach*. San Francisco: John Wiley.

11

Measuring ROI for Engagement Linked to Retention Improvement

Southeast Corridor Bank

Jack J. Phillips and Patti P. Phillips

This case was prepared to serve as a basis for discussion rather than to illustrate either effective or ineffective administrative and management practices. All names, dates, places, and organizations have been disguised at the request of the author or organization.

Abstract

This case study demonstrates how a retention improvement program at a regional bank generated an extremely significant impact, including an impressive return on investment, using a strategic accountability approach to managing retention. By analyzing the turnover problem in branch bank operations, this case focuses on how the specific causes of turnover were determined, how the solutions were matched to the special causes, and how the calculation of the actual impact of the turnover reduction was developed. The strength of the case lies in the techniques used to ensure that the solutions were appropriate and that the turnover reduction represented a high-payoff solution.

BACKGROUND

Southeast Corridor Bank (SCB), a regional bank operating in four states with 60 branches, grew from a one-state operation to a multistate network through a progressive strategic campaign of acquisitions. As a result of its growth, the bank faced merger and integration problems, including excessive employee turnover: SCB's annual turnover was 57 percent, compared with an industry average of 26 percent. When he joined SCB, the new senior vice president for human resources (SVPHR) was faced with several important challenges, among them the need to reduce turnover. Although management was not aware of the full impact of turnover, it knew turnover was causing operational problems, taking up staff and supervisor time, and creating disruptive situations for customers.

A STRATEGIC ACCOUNTABILITY APPROACH

Retention was a strategic issue for SCB because it makes the difference between mediocre and excellent profits. Thus, accountability was built into the process, allowing management to fully understand the cost of the problem, the cost of the solutions, the potential impact of the solutions, and the actual impact of the solutions, all in monetary terms. To uncover the causes of turnover, the strategic accountability approach, outlined in Exhibit 11-1, became the basic model for this case study.

This approach moves logically through a series of eight steps necessary to manage the process. It's easy to stay on track because, for the most part, each step has to be completed before moving to the next. This approach brings structure, organization, and accountability to the process, and helps organizations avoid implementing solutions without analysis.

EXHIBIT 11-1. Strategic Accountability Approach to Managing Retention

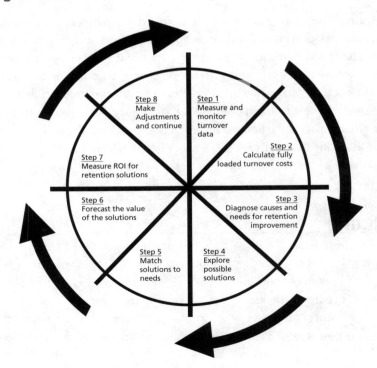

Step 1. Measure and Monitor Turnover Data

To properly monitor and measure turnover, there are several important steps:

- Define turnover consistently.
- Report turnover rates by various demographics.
- Report rates by critical job groups.
- Include costs of turnover.
- Compare turnover data with benchmarking targets.
- Develop trigger points that stimulate action.

Step 2. Calculate Fully Loaded Turnover Costs

The cost of turnover is one of the most underestimated and undervalued measures. It is often misunderstood because it is not fully loaded and does not reflect how much turnover actually costs a company. In addition, the impact of turnover is not regularly reported to the management team, keeping its members in the dark about the actual costs. However, when fully loaded costs of an organization's turnover are calculated for an entire year, the numbers can be extremely surprising.

When exploring turnover, the costs for recruiting, selecting, and training are typically considered because they are easily calculated. However, other costs are required to provide an accurate picture of the cost of turnover. A more comprehensive list includes 12 categories. The first seven are investments that are lost to some degree when an employee leaves:

- exit expense
- recruiting expense
- employment expense
- orientation expense
- training expense
- wage and salary expense while training
- temporary replacement expense.

The other five are related to the effect of turnover on conducting business:

- lost productivity
- quality problems
- customer dissatisfaction
- loss of expertise and knowledge
- loss of management time because of turnover.

Step 3. Diagnose Causes and Needs for Retention Improvement

Some causes of turnover may be obvious, but others can be extremely elusive. Collecting the appropriate data is often a challenge because of the potential for bias and the inaccuracies that can surface during data collection. Fortunately, a number of diagnostic processes are available, including:

- demographic analysis
- diagnostic instruments and mind mapping
- focus groups and brainstorming
- probing interviews
- job satisfaction and organizational commitment surveys
- exit interviews and surveys
- nominal group technique
- cause-and-effect diagrams and affinity diagrams
- force field analysis.

Step 4. Explore Possible Solutions

Many organizations are very creative in their approaches to retention problems, resulting in hundreds of excellent solutions. The critical point is to ensure that the solution is feasible for the organization. Most solutions fall into one of these categories:

- offering a competitive total compensation package that includes salary, benefits, bonuses, incentives, awards, and recognition
- building a great place to work, which champions teamwork, a healthy work environment, a supportive culture, and enabling systems
- providing growth opportunities, such as work design, empowerment, career path development, training, and succession planning
- creating a compelling future by creating a profitable organization with a competitive advantage, and developing a compelling mission, vision, and values.

Step 5. Match Solutions to Needs

This step is related to step 6, the need to forecast the value of the solutions. These two steps should be taken together because the solutions selected are assumed to meet specific needs, making the forecast of their anticipated value imperative. When attempting to match solutions to needs, consider these five key concerns:

- Avoid mismatches.
- Only implement a minimum number of solutions.
- Select a solution for a maximum return.
- Verify the match early.
- Check the progress of each solution.

Step 6. Forecast the Value of the Solutions

Developing a forecast for a solution's value allows the team to establish priorities, work with a minimum number of solutions, and focus on solutions with the greatest return on investment. Difficult, and sometimes risky, forecasting is an expert estimation of what a solution should contribute. It is imperative to accumulate as much data as possible to back up the estimate and build credibility for the process. The payoff value can be developed if the percentage of expected turnover reduction can be related to it. For example, if the top cause of turnover is removed with a particular solution, what percentage of the turnover would actually be eliminated? Employees may be able to help with this when data are collected about the cause of turnover. This step may require several "what if" decisions that may result in various assumptions. This step may also involve building on previous experiences; in some cases, the experiences of other organizations can be helpful.

Step 7. Measure ROI for Retention Solutions

Another often-neglected step is calculating the actual financial impact of a turnover reduction strategy. This step is often omitted because it appears to be unnecessary. If accumulating a number of solutions is the only measure of success of turnover reduction or prevention, the impact of those solutions may be unimportant. But from a senior executive's point of view, accountability at least for major solutions is not complete until impact and ROI data have been collected. The ROI Methodology generates six types of data about the success of a turnover reduction strategy:

- reaction to and satisfaction with the solution
- skill and knowledge acquisition
- application and implementation progress
- business impact improvement
- return on investment, expressed as an ROI formula
- intangible measures not converted to monetary values.

Step 8. Make Adjustments and Continue

The extensive set of data collected from the strategic accountability approach provides information for making adjustments and changes in turnover reduction strategies. It reveals the success of the turnover reduction solution at all levels, from reaction to ROI. It also examines barriers to success, specifically identifying what kept the solution from being effective or prevented it from becoming more effective. The approach also identifies the processes that enable or support a turnover reduction solution. This information helps determine whether the solution needs to be revised, discontinued, or amplified.

The next step in the process goes back to the beginning, monitoring the data to ensure that turnover levels continue to meet expectations . . . and the cycle continues.

MEASURING AND MONITORING TURNOVER

SCB monitored turnover in two categories, defining employee departures as either voluntary separations or terminations for performance. A voluntary termination occurred when an employee resigned voluntarily. A termination for performance involved an important problem that might have been rectified if the performance deficiency had been recognized or prevented. Departures due to retirement or disability were not included in either definition.

The turnover rate was monitored by job group, region, and bank branch. Branches had the highest turnover, averaging 71 percent in the previous year, which far exceeded any expectations or industry averages acquired from other financial institutions and the American Bankers Association. Turnover was also considered excessive in a few entry-level clerical job classifications in regional and corporate offices.

Impact of Turnover

The impact of turnover was determined at the beginning of the study. External turnover studies in the banking industry showed fully loaded turnover costs for that year ranging from 75 percent to 125 percent of annual pay (Phillips and Edwards 2009). The fully loaded costs were developed using the 12 cost categories listed in step 2. When reviewing the proposed program, the senior executive team suggested using the lower value for calculating the payoff (75 percent or 0.75 times an employee's annual pay) because it believed that turnover wasn't quite that expensive.

Determining the Cause of Turnover

Three basic techniques were used to pinpoint the actual cause of turnover. First, individual job groups and tenure within job groups were analyzed to give insight into where the turnover was occurring, the magnitude of the problem, and some indication of the cause. It was determined that much of the turnover occurred in the first six to 18 months of employment. Second, exit interviews with departing employees were examined to see if specific reasons for departure could be pinpointed. Accuracy was a concern with the exit data, as departing employees may give incomplete and inaccurate data when reporting their reasons for leaving in an effort to avoid burning bridges. Finally, the HR team used the nominal group technique to more precisely determine the actual causes of turnover.

Nominal Group Technique

The nominal group technique was selected because it allowed unbiased input to be collected efficiently and accurately across the organization. The team planned a focus group with 12 employees in each region, for a total of six groups representing all regions. In addition, two focus groups were planned for the clerical staff in corporate headquarters. This approach provided approximately a 10 percent sample, which was considered a sufficient number to pinpoint the problem.

Participants in the focus groups, who represented the areas in which turnover was highest, described why they believed their colleagues were leaving, not why they themselves would leave. Data were taken from individuals in a carefully structured format during two-hour meetings at each location, using third-party facilitators, and were integrated and weighted so the most important reasons were clearly identified. This process had the advantages of being low cost and highly reliable, as well as having a low degree of bias. Only two days of external facilitator time was needed to collect and summarize data for review.

The nominal group technique unfolded quickly in 10 steps:

1. The process steps were briefly described along with a statement of confidentiality. The importance of the participants' input was underscored so that they understood the consequences for the bank.

2. Participants were asked to list specific reasons why they believed their colleagues had left the bank or why others might leave. It was stressed that the question dealt with the actions or potential actions of employees other than themselves, although the bank realized that the participants' comments would probably reflect their own views (which were what was actually needed).

3. In a round-robin format, each person revealed one reason for turnover, which was then recorded on a flipchart. At this point, no attempt was made to integrate the issues, just to record the data. The list, containing as many as 50 or 60 items, was displayed on the walls.

4. The next step was to consolidate and integrate the list. Integration was easy when items contained the same words and meanings. However, it was important to ensure that the real reason behind the cause was the same before items were consolidated. (When this process was complete the list might have contained 30 or 40 different reasons for turnover.)

5. Participants were then asked to review all the items, carefully select those they considered to be the top 10 causes, and list them individually on index cards.

6. Next, participants ranked their top 10 items by importance, with the first item as the most important.

7. In a round-robin format, each individual revealed his number 1 item, and 10 points were recorded next to it on the flipchart. Next, the number 2 reason was identified, and nine points were recorded on the flipchart next to the item. This process continued until all reasons had been revealed and points recorded.

8. After the numbers next to each item were totaled, it was determined that the item with the most points was the leading cause of turnover. The cause with the second-highest number of points was deemed the second most important cause of turnover, and so on, until the top 15 causes were captured from that group.

9. This process was completed for all six regional groups and the two clerical staff groups; trends began to emerge quickly from one group to the next.

10. The actual raw scores were then combined to integrate the results of the six regional focus groups and the two clerical groups.

The top 15 scores represented the top 15 reasons for turnover across all the branches and clerical groups.

Specific Needs

The following list shows the top 10 causes of turnover in the bank branches:

- lack of opportunity for advancement
- lack of opportunity to learn new skills and new product knowledge
- pay level not adequate
- not enough responsibility and empowerment
- lack of recognition and appreciation of work
- lack of teamwork in the branch
- lack of preparation for customer service problems
- unfair and unsupportive supervisor
- too much stress at peak times
- not enough flexibility in work schedules.

A similar list was developed for the clerical staff, but the remainder of this case study focuses directly on the efforts to reduce turnover in the branch network.

Branch turnover was the most critical issue because it involved the highest turnover rates and the largest number of employees, and the focus group results provided a clear pattern of specific needs. Recognizing that not all causes of turnover could be addressed immediately, the bank's management set out to work on the top eight reasons while it considered a variety of options to address stress and work flexibility. These top eight reasons are representative of classic engagement requirements for employees, as reported in the Gallup Twelve Questions and Surveys from the Great Place to Work Institute as well as many other surveys.

Increasing salaries in proportion to increased responsibilities links monetary rewards to employee engagement. Consequently, jobs were redesigned, the promotion and advancement system was radically changed, and the compensation system was adjusted to allow for pay increases to become more "engaged."

SOLUTION: ENGAGEMENT LINKED WITH A REWARD

An improved employee engagement system addressed the top eight reasons for turnover, particularly when a salary increase was attached. The program was designed to expand the scope of the employees' jobs and responsibilities, with increases in pay for acquiring skills, and to provide a clear path for advancement and improvement. Jobs were redesigned from narrowly focused teller duties to an expanded job with a new classification: banking representative I, II, or III. The job descriptions were revised to provide more empowerment, teamwork, and innovation in decision making. Exhibit 11-2 shows the basic job duties for each level. Having employees perform multiple tasks was expected to broaden their responsibilities and empower them to provide excellent customer service. Pay increases were put in place to recognize skill acquisition, demonstrated accomplishment, and increased responsibility as the employees became more engaged.

EXHIBIT 11-2. Proposed Job Levels

Banking Representative Level	Job Duties
I	Basic teller transactions (e.g., deposits and check cashing)
II	Same as above, plus opening and closing accounts and processing CDs, savings bonds, special transactions, and so on
III	Same as above, plus processing limited liability consumer loans, applications for all consumer loans, referrals for mortgage loans, and so on

A branch employee would be a banking representative I if she could perform one or two simple tasks, such as processing deposits and cashing checks. As an employee at the banking representative I level took on additional responsibilities and performed different functions, she would be eligible for a promotion to banking representative II. If the representative could perform all the basic functions of the branch bank, including processing consumer loan applications, a promotion to banking representative III was appropriate. Training opportunities and self-study information was available to help employees develop the necessary job-related skills, and structured on-the-job training was also provided through the branch managers, assistant managers, and supervisors.

Although increased engagement had some definite benefits from the employee's perspective, there were also benefits for the bank. Not only was turnover expected to decrease, but actual staffing levels were expected to be reduced in larger branches. In theory, if a branch's employees could all perform every duty, then fewer employees would be needed. Prior to this time, minimum staffing levels were required in certain critical jobs, and those employees were not always available for other duties.

In addition, the bank hoped to provide an improved customer service experience, because the new approach would prevent customers from having to wait in long lines for specialized services. For example, it was not unusual to see long lines for such special functions as opening a checking account, closing out a CD, or taking a consumer loan application, whereas such activities as paying bills and receiving deposits often required little or no waiting. If each employee could perform all the tasks, shorter waiting lines would not only be feasible, but expected.

The marketing department even created a publicity campaign around this new arrangement by including a promotional piece with checking account statements introducing the concept, "In our branches there are no tellers." This document described the new process and stated that because all branch employees could perform every branch function, it would provide faster service.

Measuring Success

Measuring the success of the new solution required collecting data at four levels. At the first level, reaction and satisfaction were measured during regularly scheduled training sessions and meetings with the employees. This measurement provided input on how well employees were accepting the new arrangement and the different elements of the program. Using brief surveys, the team collected data on a five-point scale. As expected, the results were positive, averaging a 4.2 composite rating. Three important measures stood out: important to my success (4.3), I would recommend to others (4.1), and I intend to make this program successful (4.7).

At the second level, learning was measured in two different ways. Skill acquisition and knowledge increase were calculated for each training and learning opportunity, and informal self-assessments were taken for many of the programs. A few critical skills required actual demonstration to show that employees could perform them (for example, documentation, compliance, and customer services). When learning measurements revealed unacceptable performance, participants were given the opportunity to repeat training sessions or take more time to practice. In a limited number of cases, a third opportunity was provided. After one year of operation, only two employees were denied promotions based on their poor performance in training programs. The second area of learning measurements involved learning how the program works (4.2 out of 5) and how to become more engaged (4.1 out of 5).

At the third level, application and implementation were measured by collecting five types of data, as shown in Exhibit 11-3. Actual participation in the program reflected the willingness of individuals to pursue skill acquisition and increased engagement through a variety of efforts. The results were impressive.

In all, 95 percent of branch employees wanted to participate in the program. The remaining 5 percent were content with the banking representative I classification and were not interested in learning new skills. Actual requests for training and learning opportunities were a critical part of the formal process. Employees had to map out their own developmental efforts, which were then approved by the branch manager. In all, some 86 requests were logged per month, almost overtaxing the system's ability to provide training and learning opportunities.

Reviews of the status and progress—to be considered for the promotion for the next level—were significant, as this review was the formal way of demonstrating the skills required for promotion. The number of actual promotions increased quickly. As the exhibit shows, there were 139 promotions during the year before the program; this number increased to 257 during the year after the program was initiated.

The company had not used a separate engagement survey before—only a few questions on the annual feedback survey. As part of the new program, however, an engagement survey with 10 items was sent to all branch staff involved in the program six months after it began. The survey included typical engagement issues. In all, the results of the survey revealed an average of 4.1 out of 5.

Exhibit 11-3. Selected Application and Implementation Data

	1 Year Before	1 Year After
Participation in program	N/A	95%
Requests for training	45 per month	86 per month
Review Situations	N/A	138
Actual promotions	139	257
Engagement Survey	N/A	4.1

N/A = not applicable

The categories of business impact measures that were monitored are shown in Exhibit 11-4, along with their definitions. In all, nine categories of data were expected to be influenced to some degree by this project, although four—monthly branch employee turnover, staffing levels, customer satisfaction, and job satisfaction—were considered to be the primary measures.

Reduction in turnover was the most important, as that was the major thrust of the project. The company also believed that with more highly skilled and engaged employees, fewer staff should be needed, at least for the larger branches. This would be reflected in staffing levels. Customer service was expected to increase because fewer customers would be waiting in line or moving from one line to another. Job satisfaction would be reflected in employees who were more satisfied with their work, their jobs, and career possibilities.

An increase in loan volume was also expected to be attributed to the project, thanks to the decrease in the number of customers waiting in line. Consequently, customers would visit more often or would not leave in frustration because of delays. This was expected to result in an increase in the number of deposits, consumer loans, new accounts, and transactions, as well as increases in successful cross-selling. However, these last five categories were measures of each branch and were expected to move very little because of this project.

Exhibit 11-4. Business Measures Influenced by the Project

Business Impact Measures	Definitions
Branch employee turnover (monthly)	Avoidable turnover (total number of employees leaving voluntarily and for performance reasons divided by the average number of employees in the branch for the month); this number was multiplied by 12 to develop the annual turnover rate
Staffing level	The total number of employees in the branch, reported monthly
Customer satisfaction	Customer reaction to the job changes (faster service, fewer lines) measured on a 5-point scale
Job satisfaction	Employee feedback on selected measures on the annual feedback survey process
Deposits	Savings, checking, and security deposits by type and product
Loan volume	Consumer loan volume by loan type
New accounts	New accounts opened for new customers
Transaction volume	Number of face-to-face transactions, paying and receiving, by major category
Cross-selling	New products sold to existing customers

Isolating the Effects of the Project

In almost any situation, multiple influences will affect specific business measures, so it's important to isolate the actual impact of the engagement program from other influences. To add credibility and validity to the analysis, the team used estimates from branch managers and staff to isolate the effects of the project for each data item used in the ROI calculation (Exhibit 11-5). In brief group meetings, the staff were told the actual results of the turnover reduction and asked to allocate what percentage of the reduction was linked directly to the engagement effort. Each branch provided this information.

Branch team members also discussed whether any other factors could have contributed to turnover reduction (only two were identified). Then, in a focus group format, they were asked to discuss the link between each factor and the actual turnover reduction. This improved the accuracy of the estimation. The team also added an error adjustment to the estimates: Individuals were asked to indicate the level of confidence in their estimate using a scale of 0 to 100 percent, with 0 percent meaning no confidence and 100 percent meaning absolute certainty. This number was used to discount that employee's allocation. For example, if an individual allocated 60 percent of the turnover reduction to this specific project and was 80 percent confident in that allocation, the adjusted value would be 48 percent ($.06 \times .08 = 0.48$). This method of isolation provided a conservative estimate for the effect of the program on turnover reduction.

Branch managers were asked to calculate improvements in staffing levels. As before, branch managers indicated the degree to which the engagement program had resulted in actual staff reductions. However, staff reductions had only occurred in the larger branches, so this estimate only involved those branch managers. Because no other factors seemed to have contributed to the staff reduction, credit for the entire reduction was given to the program.

Exhibit 11-5 shows the method for isolating each measure that was a part of the planning for the study. Increases in deposits, loan volume, new accounts, transactions, and cross-selling were minimal and influenced by many variables other than the new program, so no attempt was made to isolate the effect or to use them in the ROI analysis. However, they were reported as intangibles to provide evidence that they were, at least to some degree, affected by the turnover reduction program.

EXHIBIT 11-5. Business Measures and Planned Analysis

Data Item	Method of Isolating the Effects	Method of Converting Data
Employee turnover	Branch manager and staff estimation	External studies
Staffing levels	Branch manager estimation	Company payroll records
Customer service	Customer input	N/A
Job satisfaction	Staff input	N/A
Deposits, loan volume, new accounts	Branch manager estimation	Standard value (percent margin)
Transaction volume, cross-selling	Branch manager and staff estimation	Standard value (average percent margin)

Customer reactions were provided by survey cards, which the customer could complete at the end of a transaction and deposit at the entrance to the branch. The customers appreciated the new approach, liked the service delivered, and indicated that they would continue to use the branch. The annual employee job satisfaction survey showed that employees were pleased with the improvements in advancement opportunities, the chance to use skills, performance-based pay, and other related engagement issues. Because customer service and job satisfaction measures were not isolated or converted to monetary value, they were not used in the ROI calculation. However, these measures were very important and influential in the final evaluation and were listed as intangible benefits.

Converting Data

Exhibit 11-5 also shows the method used (or planned) to convert data to monetary value. Turnover was converted to monetary value starting with a value from external studies. The specific amount of one turnover was calculated using 0.9 multiplied by the annual salary. This value—developed and agreed to in a meeting with senior management during the planning phase of the project—was conservative; other studies used values ranging from .75 to 1.25 multiplied by annual earnings. Because the average annual salary of the branch bank staff was $28,200, an average savings of $21,150 was realized for each potential employee departure that was prevented ($28,200 ´ 0.75).

After one year of the engagement program, the company saw a turnover reduction of 109 (Exhibit 11-6). That number was reduced to 75 prevented turnovers after adjusting for contribution factor and confidence error, which had been obtained in branch meetings, as described earlier. Then the average cost of a turnover ($21,150) was multiplied by 75 to yield an annual value of more than $1.5 million. At that point in data collection, the second-year value was unknown, so that amount was doubled to estimate the two-year savings.

Staffing levels were initially going to be converted to a monetary value using the actual salaries for the jobs that had been eliminated. However, because only a few branches were affected, the actual number was multiplied by the average salary of the branch staff. The value was captured for one year using the same calculation process as for the turnover reduction, and then doubled to show a two-year benefit of nearly $1 million.

This program was not intended to be a short-term solution and was expected to provide extended value. However, the team used a two-year timeframe because it is a conservative way to evaluate ROI (that is, one year of actual data and a forecast of one year), and additional benefits beyond the two years were excluded.

ANALYSIS

The turnover reduction at the branches was significant, dropping from 71 percent to 35 percent in one year. Although some of the smaller branches did not see any changes in the staffing levels, the larger branches did have fewer staff members after a year. In all, 30 percent of the branches were able to reduce part-time or full-time staff levels by at least one member; 10 percent of the branches were able to reduce staff by two individuals.

As shown in Exhibit 11-6 and outlined in the previous section, the total two-year benefits of the employee engagement program reached just over $3 million, with an addition savings of nearly $1 million in staffing levels.

EXHIBIT 11-6. Calculation of Actual Business Results

	Preceding Year	One Year After	Actual Difference	Contribution Factor	Confidence Estimate	Adjusted Amount	Unit Amount	First-Year Benefits	Two-Year Benefits
Turnover	271 (57%)	162 (35%)	109	84%	82%	75	$21,150	$1,586,250	$3,172,500
Staffing Levels	480 (average)	463 (end of year)	17	100%	100%	17	$28,200	$479,400	$ 958,800

Project Cost

Exhibit 11-7 shows the fully loaded cost of the project. The initial analysis costs were included along with the time, direct costs, and travel expenses for the focus groups. The next two items were branch staff time, which represented an estimate of all the time employees and managers had to spend away from their normal work to understand the program and learn new skills, including a session on how to engage employees. Facilities cost and travel cost for meetings are also listed. Actual salary increases—the additional salaries in the branches as a result of promotions—were calculated. The total amount of staff salary increases or promotions during the first year ($977,600) was reduced by the rate of promotions that had occurred in the year before the program was implemented. This accounts for the change only.

The ongoing administration and operation costs involved the time required for the HR staff to administer the program. Finally, the evaluation costs represented the costs related to developing the study of the project's effect on the business. The total cost presented in this exhibit includes several items that were involved only in the first year's actual cost one-year forecast; these costs are the totals for the project in those categories. Across all categories for two years, the total cost of the program is $941,596 + $433,200 = $1,374,796.

Exhibit 11-7. Fully Loaded Project Costs

Project Costs	Year 1	Year 2
Initial analysis	$14,000	---
Program development	$22,500	---
Branch staff time	$345,600	$195,000
Branch manager time	$40,800	$30,200
Facilities	$35,000	
Travel	$17,000	
Salary increases	$446,696	$203,900
Administration/operation	$14,000	$4,100
Evaluation	$6,000	
Total:	$941,596	$433,200

Calculating BCR and ROI

The two-year monetary benefits were combined with costs to develop the BCR and the ROI. The solution benefit represents the total two-year benefits and is calculated by adding the total benefit from turnover to the total benefit from staffing levels ($3,172,500 + $958,800 = 4,131,300).

$$BCR = \frac{\text{Solution Benefits}}{\text{Solution Cost}} = \frac{\$4,131,300}{\$1,374,796} = 3.01$$

$$BCR = \frac{\text{Net Solution Benefits}}{\text{Solution Cost}} = \frac{\$4,131,300 - \$1,374,796}{\$1,374,796} \times 100 = 201\%$$

This BCR value indicates that for every $1 invested in the project, $3.01 is returned. In terms of ROI, for every $1 invested, $2.01 is returned after the costs are captured. These results are excellent, since the ROI objective was 25 percent. The ROI was only one measure and should be considered in conjunction with other measures. However, because it was developed using a conservative approach, the ROI probably underestimated the actual return from this project.

COMMUNICATING RESULTS

The results were communicated to the senior management team in an executive staff meeting, during which approximately 30 minutes were allocated to the project report. The discussion covered these points:

- The project was quickly reviewed, including the description of the solution.
- The methodology used for evaluating the project was described.
- The results were revealed one level at a time, presenting the:
  - reaction of employees to the engagement program
  - learning the system and how to use it
  - application of the system
  - business impact of engagement
  - ROI in engagement
  - intangible measures linked to engagement.

This presentation provided a balanced profile of the project and was convincing to the senior management team. This was the first time an HR solution to a problem had been evaluated using a balanced measurement approach that included ROI. The intangible measures also were important, particularly the improvement in customer service. Overall, the senior management team was very pleased with the success of the project and impressed with the analysis.

LESSONS LEARNED

Although this project arrived at the right solution, a few lessons were learned. First, because forecasting is such an important step in the strategic accountability approach to managing retention, it may have been safer to forecast the ROI at the time the solution was developed. In particular, increasing the branch salaries to the extent planned for this solution was risky: It would have been difficult to retract this program had it not shown enough value to make it worthwhile. In addition, the branch and regional managers were not entirely convinced that improving employee engagement would add value, and additional effort was needed to capture their buy-in and help them understand the full cost of turnover. They needed to see how this system could alleviate many of their problems and add monetary value to the branches. A forecasted ROI could have provided more confidence before the program was put in place, but although this was considered, it was not pursued.

Finally, the team should have better estimated the time required of branch managers, who had to deal with numerous requests for training and juggle schedules to ensure the staff received the training they needed. The managers also had to provide additional training sessions and spend time assessing whether the bank representatives had obtained the skills necessary for promotion.

QUESTIONS FOR DISCUSSION

1. This case study illustrates how the actual causes of turnover were determined. What is your reaction to this process?
2. Why do many organizations spend so little time determining the causes of turnover?
3. Calculating the ROI of an engagement program is rarely done, yet it can have tremendous benefits. Why is this step often omitted?
4. How can the data from this project be used in the future?
5. Critique the overall approach to this project, highlighting weaknesses and strengths.

REFERENCES

Buckingham, M., and C. Coffman. 1999. *First Break All the Rules: What the World's Greatest Managers Do Differently*. New York: Simon & Schuster.

Phillips, J.J., and L. Edwards. 2009. *Managing Talent Retention: An ROI Approach*. San Francisco: Pfeiffer.

Phillips, P.P., and J.J. Phillips. 2015. *Real World Training Evaluation: Navigating Common Constraints for Exceptional Results*. Alexandria, VA: ATD Press.

About ROI Institute

ROI Institute is the leading resource on research, training, and networking for practitioners of the Phillips ROI Methodology.

With a combined 50 years of experience in measuring and evaluating training, human resources, technology, and quality programs and initiatives, Jack J. Phillips, PhD, chairman, and Patti P. Phillips, PhD, president, are the leading experts in return on investment.

ROI Institute, founded in 1992, is a service-driven organization that strives to assist professionals in improving their programs and processes through the use of the ROI Methodology. Developed by Jack Phillips, this methodology is a critical tool for measuring and evaluating programs in 18 different applications in more than 60 countries.

ROI Institute offers a variety of consulting services, learning opportunities, and publications. In addition, it conducts internal research activities for the organization, other enterprises, public sector entities, industries, and interest groups. Together with their team, Jack and Patti Phillips serve private and public sector organizations globally.

BUILD CAPABILITY IN THE ROI METHODOLOGY

ROI Institute offers a variety of workshops to help you build capability through the ROI Methodology. Among the many workshops offered through the institute are:

- A one-day *Bottomline on ROI* Workshop, which provides the perfect introduction to all levels of measurement, including the most sophisticated level, ROI. Learn the key principles of the Phillips ROI Methodology and determine whether your organization is ready to implement the process.
- A two-day *ROI Competency Building* Workshop, which is the standard ROI workshop on measurement and evaluation. This two-day program involves discussion of the ROI Methodology process, including data collection, isolation methods, data conversion, and more.

ROI CERTIFICATION

ROI Institute is the only organization offering certification in the ROI Methodology. Through the ROI Certification process, you can build expertise in implementing ROI evaluation and sustaining the measurement and evaluation process in your organization. Receive personalized coaching while conducting an impact study. When competencies in the ROI Methodology have been demonstrated, certification is awarded. There is not another process that provides access to the same level of expertise as our ROI Certification. To date, more than 10,000 individuals have participated in this process.

For more information on these and other workshops, learning opportunities, consulting, and research, please visit us on the Web at **www.roiinstitute.net**, or call us at **205.678.8101.**

About the Authors

Jack J. Phillips, PhD, is a world-renowned expert on accountability, measurement, and evaluation. Phillips provides consulting services for Fortune 500 companies and major global organizations. The author or editor of more than 50 books, he conducts workshops and presents at conferences throughout the world.

Phillips has received several awards for his books and work. On three occasions, Meeting News named him one of the 25 Most Powerful People in the Meetings and Events Industry, based on his work on ROI. The Society for Human Resource Management presented him with an award for one of his books and honored a Phillips ROI study with its highest award for creativity. The Associaton for Talent Development gave him its highest award, Distinguished Contribution to Workplace Learning and Development, for his work on ROI. His work has been featured in the *Wall Street Journal, Businessweek,* and *Fortune* magazine. He has been interviewed by several television outlets, including CNN. Phillips served as president of the International Society for Performance Improvement, 2012-2013.

His expertise in measurement and evaluation is based on more than 27 years of corporate experience in the aerospace, textile, metals, construction materials, and banking industries. Phillips has served as training and development manager at two Fortune 500 firms, as senior human resource officer at two firms, as president of a regional bank, and as a management professor at a major state university.

This background led Phillips to develop the ROI Methodology, a revolutionary process that provides bottom-line figures and accountability for all types of learning, performance improvement, human resource, technology, and public policy programs.

Phillips regularly consults with clients in manufacturing, service, and government organizations in more than 60 countries in North and South America, Europe, Africa, Australia, and Asia.

Phillips has undergraduate degrees in electrical engineering, physics, and mathematics; a master's degree in decision sciences from Georgia State University; and a PhD in human resource management from the University of Alabama. He has served on the boards of several private businesses—including two NASDAQ companies—and several nonprofits and associations, including the Associaton for Talent Development and the National Management Association. He is chairman of ROI Institute and can be reached at 205.678.8101, or by email at jack@roiinstitute.net.

 **Patti Phillips, PhD,** is president and CEO of ROI Institute, the leading source of ROI competency building, implementation support, networking, and research. A renowned expert in measurement and evaluation, she helps organizations implement the ROI Methodology in more than 60 countries around the world.

Since 1997, following a 13-year career in the electric utility industry, Phillips has embraced the ROI Methodology by committing herself to ongoing research and practice. To this end, she has implemented ROI in private sector and public sector organizations. She has conducted ROI impact studies on programs such as leadership development, sales, new-hire orientation, human performance improvement, K-12 educator development, and educators' National Board Certification mentoring.

Phillips teaches others to implement the ROI Methodology through the ROI Certification process, as a facilitator for ATD's ROI and Measuring and Evaluating Learning Workshops, and as professor of practice for the University of Southern Mississippi Gulf Coast Campus PhD in human capital development program. She also serves as adjunct faculty for the UN System Staff College in Turin, Italy, where she teaches the ROI Methodology through its Evaluation and Impact Assessment Workshop and Measurement for Results-Based Management. She serves on numerous doctoral dissertation committees, assisting students as they develop their own research on measurement, evaluation, and ROI.

Phillips's academic accomplishments include a PhD in international development and a master's degree in public and private management. She is a certified in ROI evaluation and has been awarded the designations of Certified Professional in Learning and Performance and Certified Performance Technologist. Patti Phillips can be reached at patti@roiinstitute.net.

Jack and Patti Phillips contribute to a variety of journals and have authored a number of books on the subject of accountability and ROI, including *Real World Evaluation Training* (ATD Press 2016); *High Impact Human Capital Strategy* (AMACOM 2015); *Maximizing the Value of Consulting* (Wiley 2015); *Performance Consulting*, 3rd ed. (Berrett Koehler 2015); *Measuring the Success of Leadership Development* (ATD Press 2015); *Making Human Capital Analytics Work* (McGraw-Hill 2015); *Measuring ROI in Environment, Health, and Safety* (Wiley 2014); *Measuring the Success of Learning Through Technology* (ASTD Press 2014); *Measuring the Success of Organization Development* (ASTD Press 2013); *Survey Basics* (ASTD Press 2013); *Measuring the Success of Sales Training* (ASTD Press 2013); *Measuring ROI in Healthcare* (McGraw-Hill 2012); *Measuring the Success of Coaching* (ASTD Press 2012); *Measuring Leadership Development: Quantify your Program's Impact and ROI on Organizational Performance* (McGraw-Hill 2012); *10 Steps to Successful Business Alignment* (ASTD Press 2011); *The Green Scorecard: Measuring the Return on Investment in Sustainability Initiatives* (Nicholas Brealey 2011); and *Project Management ROI* (John Wiley 2011). Patti and Jack have also served as authors and series editors for the Measurement and Evaluation Series published by Pfeiffer (2008), which includes six books on the ROI Methodology and a companion book of 14 best-practice case studies.

Rebecca Ray, PhD, is executive vice president, knowledge organization and human capital practice lead for The Conference Board. In this role, she has oversight of the research planning and dissemination process for three practice areas: corporate leadership, economics and business development, and human capital. She is the leader of the global human capital practice.

Rebecca was previously a senior executive responsible for talent acquisition, organizational learning, training, management and leadership development, employee engagement, performance management, executive assessment, coaching, organization development, and succession planning at several major companies. She taught at Oxford and New York Universities, and led a consulting practice for many years, offering leadership assessment and development services to Fortune 500 companies and top-tier professional services firms. Rebecca was named Chief Learning Officer of the Year by *Chief Learning Officer* magazine, and one of the Top 100 People in Leadership Development by Warren Bennis's *Leadership Excellence* magazine. She serves on the advisory boards for New York University's program in higher education and business education at the Steinhardt School of Education and the University of Pennsylvania's executive program in work-based learning leadership. She was elected to serve on the Business Practices Council of the AACSB (Association to Advance Collegiate Schools of Business).

Rebecca received a PhD from New York University and is a frequent speaker at professional and company-sponsored conferences and business briefings around the world. She is the co-author of numerous publications on leadership development, analytics, and engagement, including *Measuring the Success of Leadership Development* (ATD Press 2015) and *Measuring Leadership Development* (McGraw-Hill 2012).

Index